THE
CUMBRIA
WAY

Also available
The Cotswold Way
The Dales Way
The Saxon Shore Way
The West Highland Way
The Southern Upland Way
The Two Moors Way
The Heart of England Way
The Wye Valley Walk
The Wessex Ridgeway

RECREATIONAL PATH GUIDE

THE
CUMBRIA
WAY

ANTHONY BURTON

Photographs by Rob Scott

Aurum Press

Ordnance Survey

First published 1999 by Aurum Press Limited, 25 Bedford Avenue, London, WC1B 3AT
in association with the Ordnance Survey.

A catalogue record for this book is available from the British Library.

ISBN 1 85410 615 5
Book designed by Robert Updegraff
Printed and bound in Italy by Printers Trento Srl
Cover: *Looking down Langstrath from Stake Pass*
Title Page: *The summit of Stake Pass*

CONTENTS

*Walks to the peaks of the Old Man of Coniston and Skiddaw
will be found on pages 74 and 126*

How to Use this Guide

This guide is in three parts:
· The introduction, historical background to the area and advice for walkers.
· The path itself, described in five chapters, with maps opposite each route description. This part of the guide also includes information on places of interest. Key sites are numbered in the text and on the maps to make it easy to follow the route description.
· The last part includes useful information such as local transport, accommodation, organizations involved with the path and further reading.

The maps have been prepared by the Ordnance Survey® for this guide using 1:25 000 Pathfinder® or Outdoor Leisure™ maps as a base. The line of the Cumbria Way is shown in yellow, with the status of each section of the path – footpath or bridleway, for example – shown in green underneath (see key on inside front cover). These rights of way markings also indicate the precise alignment of the path at the time of the orginal surveys, but in some cases the yellow line on these maps may show a route that is different from that shown by those older surveys, and in such cases walkers are recommended to follow the yellow route in this guide. Any parts of the path that may be difficult to follow on the ground are clearly highlighted in the route description, and important points to watch for are marked with letters in each chapter, both in the text and on the maps. *Some maps start on a right-hand page and continue on the left-hand page* – black arrows (➡) *at the edge of the maps indicate the start point.* Should there have been a need to alter the route since publication of this guide for any reason, walkers are advised to follow the waymarks or signs that have been put up on site to indicate this.

DISTANCE CHECKLIST

This list will help you in calculating the distances between places on the Cumbria Way, whether you are planning your overnight stays, or checking your progress.

Location	approximate distance from previous location	
	miles	*km*
Ulverston	0	0
Gawthwaite	5	8.0
Beacon Tarn	4	6.0
Coniston Water	2$\frac{1}{2}$	4.0
Coniston	3	5.0
Tarn Hows	2$\frac{1}{2}$	4.0
Skelwith Bridge	4	6.0
Chapel Stile	2	3.5
Old Dungeon Ghyll	2$\frac{1}{2}$	4.0
Stake Pass (top)	2$\frac{1}{2}$	4.0
Rosthwaite	5	8.5
Derwent Water	3$\frac{1}{2}$	5.5
Keswick	4	6.5
Skiddaw House	5	8.5
Nether Row (Eastern route)	8	12.5
Nether Row (Western route)	10$\frac{1}{2}$	16.5
Caldbeck	1	2.0
Sebergham church	4	6.0
Dalston	6	9.5
Carlisle	5$\frac{1}{2}$	9.0

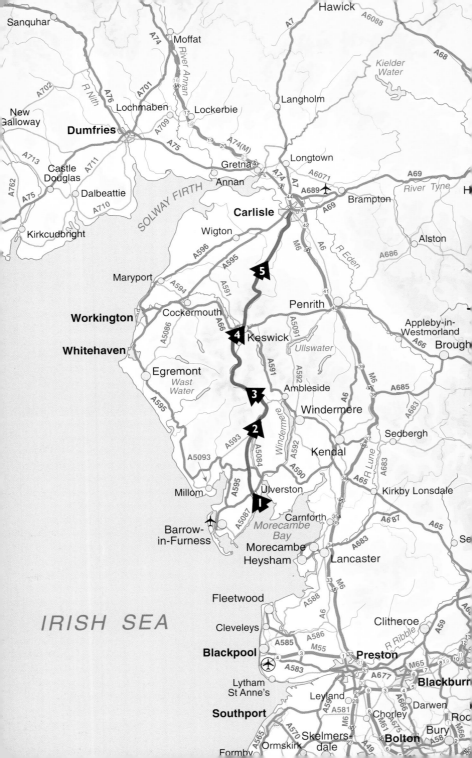

KEY MAP

Cumbria Way

2 Chapter start point

0 km 10 20

0 miles 10

INTRODUCTION

The path from Skiddaw House, leading towards the top of Whitewater Dash, with Binsey Hill in the distance.

WALKING THE CUMBRIA WAY

The first point to note is that this is the Cumbria Way not the Lake District Way, even if a large part of the walk does fall within the boundaries of the National Park. It has been designed to show the region in all its different aspects and moods, from Morecambe Bay in the south to within sight of the Solway Firth and the hills of Scotland in the north. It begins very gently, with farmland and pasture, but as the walk continues the Way gets rougher and the scenery takes on a harder edge as rocks push out to the surface and the rich green grass of pasture gives way to the pallid spiky clumps of moorland. Then the first of the lakes is reached with its dramatic setting of craggy hills, and the promise of ever wilder walks across the high hills. Lakeland grandeur appears at its finest with the climb out of the Langdale valley and the crossing of the watershed to look out over lonely Langstrath and the entrance to Borrowdale. Yet another change of mood occurs beyond Keswick as the way stretches out over the more rounded fells, for what can be the loneliest, most remote and wildest section of the whole walk. Then the fells come to an end and the Cumbria Way returns to ever richer farmland as it follows the wanderings of the River Caldew to the ancient border city of Carlisle. No one walking the Cumbria Way could ever complain of lack of variety.

Walkers setting out along the way have to decide the direction in which they are to go, and in this case there is no obvious answer. Both ends of the walk are easily reached by public transport. The prevailing winds are westerlies, and so will blow across the route whether one is walking north to south or vice versa. The disadvantage of starting in the south is that if the wind should swing to the north it is likely to bring cold weather driving straight into your face. To set against that, in good weather it is always more pleasant to have the sun on your back rather than glaring into your eyes. There is virtually no difference in difficulty: you have a stiff climb to face in crossing

Stake Pass, for example, whichever way you choose to travel. In this book, the description is for a northward walk beginning at Ulverston, and the choice was made for what might seem rather subjective reasons, but walks also tend to have a shape which is somehow more satisfying when seen in one way rather than another. In heading north, the fells seem to creep up on one gradually, building a pattern of ever more rugged and higher hills. If one starts in the north, the hills rise up quite suddenly, making an absolute break between two very different landscapes. There is also a personal element. I first came to the area many years ago as a schoolboy and walked from Ambleside into the Langdale valley and can still recall the extraordinary beauty of the Pikes silhouetted against a steadily darkening sky. Then in daylight to climb up Stake Pass and see the whole majesty of the mountains spread out all around was an experience I have never forgotten. It seemed to me then the perfect introduction to the high fells and it still seems so today. So, instinctively almost, I decided that south to north, Ulverston to Carlisle it had to be.

This is not an excessively demanding walk, but it is most definitely a walk to be taken seriously, particularly when crossing the high ground. Climbing up to both Stake Pass and the Caldbeck fells is likely to bring you above the cloud base on a bad day, and there can be some very bad days indeed in this area. The weather is notoriously fickle, so that one has to be prepared for any eventuality, whatever the time of year. Each season has its own appeal and its own disadvantages. Spring brings the daffodils, but snow may linger on the tops; summer, with luck, brings the sun, but also the crowds to popular centres such as Coniston, Keswick and Langdale: autumn can be majestic, but can also be cold and wet. Winter, however, is a different matter altogether. Whatever the conditions in the valleys, there is every chance of meeting fierce weather with snow and ice on the tops. Only those fully equipped for serious winter walking and experienced in snow conditions should consider setting off on the Way during these months.

Whatever the season, it is important to be properly prepared and equipped. Many sections of the way go for long distances through tracts of wild countryside with virtually nothing in the way of shelter, and one has always to remember that even climbing a thousand feet above the valley floor can produce a dramatic change. Whilst walking the route in order to prepare this book, I left Keswick on a pleasant, mercifully dry day, but by the time I reached the top of High Peak I was almost blown off the summit by a gale-force wind. So good weatherproof clothing is an absolute essential, and this is very defi-

Dramatic waterfalls are very much a feature of the Cumbria Way. This is Whitewater Dash on the western route from Skiddaw.

The route above Derwent Water provides an appealing mixture of grassy farmland and

ough-hewn hills.

Some of the most rugged scenery on the whole route is to be found in the section between Langdale and Borrowdale. This is Stonethwaite Beck.

nitely a route that calls for boots, not shoes or, worse still, trainers. Much of the way lies along rough, stony tracks and there are steep descents where good ankle support is really necessary. There are countless streams to be crossed and there are some places where, in wet weather, the path itself almost turns into a stream. The main object of going on such a walk is enjoyment, and there is not much fun in being soaked to the skin with sodden feet: keep yourself warm and dry and even the worst conditions are tolerable. Whilst most of us would opt for a fine sunny day there is even a special sort of grim pleasure in being out on the hills when the clouds hang down ragged curtains of rain and the crags glisten and stream with water: it is rather like changing Mozart for Wagner. Equally, there is not much fun in being hungry and thirsty. There are long sections of empty countryside along the way, with nowhere to stop for snacks or lunch, so make sure you carry enough food and, even more importantly, drink for a full day's walk.

One other vital factor has to be taken into consideration, safety. Many walking guides suggest a minimum of three to a party. Then, if there is an accident, that leaves one to stay with the injured and the third to go for help. This is very sound advice, but not everyone chooses to walk in parties at all – over the past few years I have walked literally thousands of miles on long distance paths nearly always on my own. There is nothing wrong with this, provided one takes sensible precautions, and knows what one is doing. The first essential is to make sure somebody knows where you are going and when you are likely to reach your destination – search parties only go looking for people if they know they are missing. And if things do go wrong, you want to be found as soon as possible – the most useful thing for attracting attention is a good loud whistle. But by far the best way to ensure your safety is to make certain that things do not go wrong in the first place, and usually problems involve getting lost. The object of writing this book is, of course, to help avoid that happening, but even so mistakes can be made. Unlike many long distance paths, the Cumbria Way is not regularly waymarked, and there are many areas, notably the fells beyond Skiddaw House, where paths are indistinct or even non-existent. The southern end of the walk presents different problems, a complex route being threaded through farmland. The book provides all the route maps you need but there is not much use having a map unless you know which way you are going and that means carrying a compass and knowing how to use it. This is particularly important in the uplands. The way is inevitably described in terms of landmarks, but in mist or low cloud these may not be visible, and then the compass is not just useful but essential. It is possible to reduce the chances of being caught with really poor visibility. Later in the book, you will find a choice of routes between Skiddaw House and Caldbeck, and it really is sensible to follow the advice given there and take the lower route in bad weather. Equally, the two ascents offered as extras should only be undertaken when the peaks are clear of cloud. Apart from the fact that there is not much sense in climbing a mountain when you cannot see anything, these hills can be dangerous. This is particularly true of the summit of the Old Man of Coniston with a complex of rocks, crags and sudden drops.

Writers of guides tend to stress safety, and it is absolutely right to do so, but it can give the impression that walking the Cumbria Way is a slog through endless rain storms, punctuated by aimless wandering over an empty moor desperately searching for the path, with a fracture clinic as the final destination. It is not, and certainly need not be, like that. This is a wonderfully exhilarating walk through superb scenery, which should not overtax any reasonably fit person. It is perfectly possible to walk the whole route in five days, though extra time may need to be added on by those going for one or both of the ascents. Accommodation is not a great problem. Those who are camping will find no shortage of camp sites, and bed and breakfasts and hotels proliferate. It should, however, be remembered that the Lake District is an immensely popular holiday area and rooms do get booked up very quickly. There is a lot to be said for arranging rooms in advance, but, on the other hand, taking pot luck does provide flexibility – and the option of sitting out a truly horrendous day.

This is not a route invented by the author of this guide. It was pioneered by the Ramblers' Association, whose address can be found at the back of this book. They deserve the credit not just for planning such an excellent and varied walk, using a mixture of public footpaths, bridleways and open access land, but also for their continuing work in preserving rights of way and keeping paths open. Inevitably, there are changes from time to time, with footpath realignments and, at the time I walked, there had been a major diversion caused by riverbank erosion. Where diversions are signposted, they should always be observed, but hopefully they will be very few. If there are any obstructions to rights of way it would be a great help if it could be reported to the Ramblers' Association. In any case, somewhere along the Way, one should tip one's hat or raise a glass to the enthusiasts who created a superb walk through some of the finest scenery the British Isles can boast.

The final part of the Cumbria Way leaves the hills to follow the Caldew
Valley. Blood-drop emlets bloom beside the river.

THE LAKES

The essential character of any landscape depends on forces that have acted over the aeons of geological time. There are two basic types of rock in the Lake District: those formed by sedimentation and those created by volcanic eruption. The oldest of these date back to a period some 500 to 600 million years ago when the whole region was covered by a shallow sea. As the waters retreated, the mud hardened to form layers of slate which in turn were thrust up and crumpled by movements in the earth's crust. The most dramatic are the Skiddaw Slates which were thrust up to create narrow ridges and angular peaks, through which streams have carved out deep gorges. The other sedimentary rocks, formed more recently at around 400 million years ago, have created the gentler slopes at the southern end of the region round Coniston. Then, around 100 million years ago, volcanoes erupted through the area, hurling up lava which solidified to form the rocks of the major peaks of the area – The Old Man of Coniston and the Langdale Pikes among them.

Over the almost unimaginable time that has elapsed since the main elements of the landscape were created, there have been movements and erosions, but a pattern was created. The whole district can be thought of as starting as one great dome from which water ran off in every direction, creating a system of valleys radiating out like spokes from a hub. Then came the Ice Ages, lasting over a period of hundreds of thousands of years, only ending in Britain as recently as 20,000 years ago. During that time, the ice advanced and retreated, grinding away at the rocks, while the debris was carried along on the slowly moving glaciers. The most spectacular survivor is the Bowder Stone in Borrowdale, an immense boulder estimated at 2000 tonnes left perched as if it might topple at any moment. The ice cut out great troughs – the bed of Wastwater is actually some 20 metres below the level of the Irish Sea. As the ice finally melted, the troughs were filled to create the lakes, typically narrow and thin. At the northern end of Bassenthwaite Lake are huge areas of glacial deposits, while the rivers to either side have created a delta blocking the southern end, and cutting it off from Derwent Water. In other areas, small glaciers have dug out hollows in the hills, which have in time become the small tarns so typical of the upland areas.

The lakes were formed a long time ago, but their continued existence is due to a fact of which regular walkers in the area will be all too well aware: this is a region with a lot of rain. The prevailing winds sweep in from the west, picking up moisture as they cross the sea. As the airstream hits the hills, it is forced up, cooling as it rises. Cold air holds less moisture than warm air, so clouds form over the hills. Eventually, the water falls to ground as rain or snow. We may not like the rain, but without it there would be no lakes.

The lakes themselves, with their protective hills, have become immensely popular with boaters of all kinds – rowing boats and dinghies take to the water on the smaller lakes, while Coniston boasts a magnificent survivor from the Victorian age – the steam yacht *Gondola*, built in 1859 and now taking passengers to enjoy the placid waters. Not that the waters are always peaceful. Sudden squalls can roughen the surface quickly and dramatically, and it was just such a flurry that led to the death of Donald Campbell when he was attempting to break the world water speed record on Coniston in 1967. On sullen days any of the lakes can seem dark and uninviting, but when the sun glistens on the water they give the area a unique fascination and beauty.

The northern end of Derwent Water, with its wooded banks and surrounding hills epitomises the charm of the Lakes.

The rough track winds round the hillside of Cockup Fell, with Whitewater Dash falls

e background.

NATURAL HISTORY

That this is an area with a rich and varied natural history is indicated by the fact that Cumbria has more National Nature Reserves than any other county in England. Although none of them lie directly on the Way, walkers will find themselves visiting a wide range of different environments from high fells to broad-leaved woodland and, of course, lakes and tarns.

The Way starts near the coast at Ulverston, and any bird watcher who can spare a few hours before starting the walk proper should visit Morecambe Bay. In winter, up to a quarter of a million waders come to feed on the sand flats – godwits, curlew, oystercatchers and others – while the pools left by the tide attract a rich variety of wildfowl.

The lakes have their own residents. In general, the deeper, colder lakes such as Coniston, have fewer species of fish than shallower lakes such as Derwent Water. The most common species are brown trout and char. The latter, a creature with the unpleasant habit of eating its own young, is caught by a unique method, known as 'plumbline angling'. Short, strong rods with bells on top are put out to each side of the boat, trailing 70 to 80 feet (20 to 25 metres) of weighted line, to which side lines with spinners are attached. A catch is signalled by the tinkle of the bell. These waters also attract an array of waterfowl, including one or two rarer species, such as the red-breasted merganser, which breeds here, and whooper swans, which come as winter visitors. Sandpipers and grey wagtails can be seen at the water's edge, while dippers hop busily among the rocks in the adjoining streams.

The hills have a spectacular range of birds as well. Golden plover are found on the moors in summer, and the walker will be treated to two very different, but equally characteristic cries: the harsh voice of the raven echoes around the crags, while the curlew's 'coo-ee' sounds high over the fells. The red kite was common in Wordsworth's day, but has now virtually disappeared. There are, however, many other birds of prey to be seen above the hills. Along with the more common species, there are peregrine falcons, which have made a comeback in recent years, and, if one is very fortunate, it is possible to catch sight of a golden eagle.

The animals most commonly encountered are sheep, including the distinctive Herdwicks, originally brought over by the Norsemen. They are particularly well adapted to the region, as their long, coarse fleece enables them to stay on the fells right through the year. Their main source of food is sheep's fescue, though in heavily grazed areas this may be replaced by mat-grass. There are some red deer in the area,

The country lane leading to Caldbeck runs between banks rich with wild flowers and wearing a snowy crown of hawthorn.

but roe deer are more common, usually seen at dawn or in the late evening when they come out from the shelter of the woods to graze. The woods are also home to the red squirrel. This is one of the few areas in England where these attractive creatures have not been driven out by the greys.

There is one aspect of the natural history with which, thanks to Wordsworth, everyone is familiar – the springtime luxuriance of the wild daffodils. It is one of the great good fortunes for all who love this beautiful region that the sheep find the daffodil totally unpalatable, so that each year the spectacular show returns.

Water is a vital force in forming the landscape: a typical mountain stream has erod

ne rocks to create a series of falls.

Priests Mill, Caldbeck, a former water mill built in 1702 by a Rector of Caldbeck, hence its name.

RAIDERS AND INVADERS

The area covered by the Cumbria Way has seen its fair share of violence. Historical records begin with the advance of the Romans led by Julius Agricola who conquered the whole of the territory of the Brigantes in a campaign begun in AD 79. To hold what he had conquered, he built roads and established a naval base at Ravenglass. The lines of communication were protected by forts of which the most spectacular is high in the hills at Hardknott Pass. From this base he advanced into Scotland and smashed all opposition. But then he was recalled to Rome and the Scottish tribes were able to regroup. The Romans retreated and drew a line through their most important fortress at Carlisle. This became the new frontier, and the Emperor Hadrian arrived in AD 122 to supervise the construction of the great wall that was to stretch from coast to coast. Hadrian's Wall was important for just as long as the Romans remained in Britain, but by the middle of the fifth century the last of them had gone, and the period that came to be known as the Dark Ages began.

Norsemen and Danes began raiding the coast of Britain in the eighth century. They were known collectively as 'Vikings' or pirates, but were more than just the robbers and pillagers of popular legend. The Norse Vikings settled in Ireland and on the Isle of Man, and from there they made their way into North West England, where they soon established permanent homes. The pattern of small farmers or 'statesmen' that became established in the Lake District had its origins in Norse traditions, as did the practice of dividing up the holdings by drystone walls. Norse names crop up throughout the region: 'thwaite' for a clearing, 'thorpe' for a hamlet, 'ghyll', 'beck', 'tarn' and many more.

The next great wave of invaders came with the arrival of the Normans in the eleventh century. William II marched up to Carlisle in 1092 and found the old Roman fortress in ruins, but claimed it for England. It was not to be a permanent arrangement, and for 600 years Carlisle was disputed by the Scots and English. It last exchanged hands, setting Carlisle firmly under English control, in 1745, when the Duke of Cumberland recaptured it from Bonnie Prince Charlie and his retreating followers.

Borders and border controls matter a great deal to kings and politicians, but have a very different significance for the ordinary people of the area. For centuries, they ignored the frontier altogether, crossing and recrossing it in a series of cattle-stealing raids. The 'reivers', or raiders, were bold and ranged widely. There are accounts of the Scots venturing deep into the Lake District: one legendary raid saw a small army of Scots reaching Borrowdale, where they divided forces. Half returned to Scotland driving the cattle before them, while the rest guarded the retreat. The English pursued them across the border but were ambushed. There were heavy losses, and the young Graeme, son of the chieftain Ossian, died in the fighting. One form of protection was provided by the strongly fortified house which, unlike a castle, was never intended for permanent occupation. When raiders appeared, the locals gathered what possessions they could and stayed in safety until the invaders were gone. There is a fine example beside the Way at Rose Castle. Given the history of the region it is perhaps not too surprising to find that the first tourists only began to arrive in the latter part of the eighteenth century when peace was finally established.

Rose Castle. The gaunt fifteenth-century peel tower stands in front of the more comfortable house of the Bishops of Carlisle.

Carlisle Castle, begun by William II in 1092, but the present keep and gatehouse were built around 1300.

The wild scenery that inspired the Lake Poets: Langstrath Beck rushing down its rocky gorge.

LAKES AND LITERATURE

The first, and many would say the greatest, of all Lakeland writers was William Wordsworth. Born in the region, he delighted in everything it had to offer, from swimming in the Derwent to climbing the crags for birds' nests. He revelled in his 'glad animal movements', and enjoyed the pure sensual pleasures of the region.

> *The sounding cataract*
> *Haunted me like a passion; the tall rock,*
> *The mountain, and the deep and gloomy wood,*
> *Their colours and their forms, were then to me*
> *An appetite.*

It was later in his life that he added the extra dimension: when looking at the scenes he loved, he also heard 'the still, sad music of humanity'. He made his home at Grasmere with his sister Dorothy, and in her journals one can read of the everyday life of Dove Cottage, and also discover just how the sights they met on their many walks and excursions served as an inspiration. One entry describes rowing out on Rydal Water, and hearing the cry of a raven.

> It called out, and the dome of the sky seemed to echo the sound. It called again and again as it flew onwards, and the mountains gave back the sound, seeming as if from their centre; a musical bell-like answering to the bird's hoarse cry.

William described the bird and its echoing cry in Book IV of *The Excursion*. His poetry was bred out of the landscape, but made into work of great complexity by the interplay of pure description and the thoughts and emotions of the watcher with the character of the natural world. His two friends, Coleridge and Southey, were not as wholly preoccupied with the region as Wordsworth, though they came to be known collectively as the Lake Poets. Coleridge did, however, make a major contribution to the literature of hill walking with an account of an ascent of Scafell.

Wordsworth hated the growth of tourism that was already in his lifetime destroying the vast solitude of the region – and deplored the arrival of the railway. This was a view shared – and vehemently expressed – by John Ruskin. He is best known for his books on art and architecture, and was an enthusiastic supporter of the Pre-Raphaelites – an enthusiasm somewhat dimmed when Millais ran off with his wife. In 1871 he bought the house Brantwood and Coniston is now home to the Ruskin Museum. He was a great believer in the superiority of the

Not daffodils, perhaps, but a sight that would surely have delighted Wordsworth: the

view over Ullswater

old work of craftsmen, and spent a great deal of his own money on trying to revive the hand-made linen industry in the Langdale region.

Whilst Ruskin was still living at Coniston, Cyril Ransome carried his baby son, Arthur, to the top of the Old Man of Coniston. The family were to spend their summer holidays at Nibthwaite at the southern end of Coniston Water. Arthur was to return later in life, after a dramatic career as a newspaper correspondent covering the Russian Revolution – it comes as a surprise to those who only know Arthur Ransome as the most English of writers to find that his wife was Trotsky's secretary. In 1928 he came back to Coniston to stay with the Altounyan family, sharing the children's adventures and sailing with them on the lake. The children were to find themselves immortalised in the *Swallows and Amazons* series, in which many familiar Lakeland scenes can easily be identified under their fictitious names. The idyllic life enjoyed by the children stems from the same simple response to the natural world that inspired the young William Wordsworth.

There have been other writers with Lakeland connections – Tennyson was a regular visitor to Bassenthwaite, Beatrix Potter lived and wrote from her home near Hawkshead – but for many walkers one name not only has to be included, but would top any list: A. Wainwright. His walking guides, with his own illustrative sketches, are as pleasurable to read in the home as they are useful when out on the fells.

Cottages at Caldbeck.

MAN AND THE LANDSCAPE

Most of us who come to walk in the Lake District do so, in part at least, to get away from the artificialities of the modern world, to turn to a natural, wild landscape. In fact man began dramatically to change this region over 6000 years ago. At that time most of the area was covered by birch and pine forest, but research has shown that as early as 4500 BC man had made at least one small clearing for farming at the edge of Blea Tarn high above the Langdale valley. The Langdale Pikes provide the evidence to show how this was done. Walkers on the Way will have a good view from the head of the valley to the summit of Pike of Stickle, with its neat apron of scree stretching out from the crags. The rock is hard volcanic 'tuff' and the men of Neolithic times came here to quarry. The hard stone was shaped and sharpened, and the flakes that were broken off were left where they fell, so many of them that the area has become known as an 'axe factory'. It was such axes that gave the Stone Age its name, and which were used to fell the trees and clear the land. Once clear, primitive ploughshares, also made of stone, were used to prepare it for planting. Slowly but inexorably the forest vanished.

The stone axes of the Lake District were of such good quality that they were traded over a large area, turning up as far away as Hampshire and even across the Irish Sea. Later stone, especially slate, came to be seen as valuable building materials; as all the older houses of the region bear testament. One of the important centres for slate quarrying is Skelwith Bridge on the Way.

Minerals were also exploited. At Seathwaite in Borrowdale, a few miles to the west of the Way, long adits were dug into the hillside to deposits of 'wadd' or graphite, much of which then went to Keswick where it became the lead in the pencils of the Cumberland Pencil Company. The other busy and unlikely mining region was Coniston, where copper ore was extracted.

While the Lake District can fairly claim a long industrial history, the dominant activity has been agriculture. The area appealed to the early settlers precisely because the soil was thin and easily turned by primitive ploughs. But as farm machinery improved, men turned increasingly to the rich, heavy soils of the lowlands. It became harder to make a living in the region, and soon large tracts of land were bought up and the yeomen pushed into the higher dales. Sheep farming came to dominate the region, with the pasture in the valleys often broken up into a profusion of small, irregular fields. Meanwhile, the stone walls spread ever higher up the fells.

The Old Dungeon Ghyll, a long-time favourite with walkers and climbers, sits benea

e crags of the Langdale Valley.

Old crafts survive at Caldbeck: as well as the skills advertised here, there is also a working blacksmith in the building.

Everything in the Lakeland landscape can be reduced, it seems, to two main themes: deforestation and stone. The earliest farmers began to clear the land; then as minerals were exploited, trees were felled to fuel the smelters. Once the sheep arrived, they remorselessly chewed up any small saplings that tried to get a hold. As the trees went, so erosion leached out the minerals from the soil until all it would support was bracken. Stone was collected from the land, both to build the houses and the web of walls that surround them. Even then there was more stone to be cleared than could be used, and many valleys have great heaps penned in by walls. It is a land of unity, where the rock of the crags is the rock of walls, barns and houses – a land where man has adapted nature, but never quite tamed it.

THE EARLY TOURISTS AND THE PICTURESQUE

Today we take it for granted that the words 'Lake District' are more or less synonymous with 'beautiful scenery': it was not always so. When Daniel Defoe visited the region in the 1720s he noted glumly that all he could see were 'impassable hills, whose tops covered with snow, seemed to tell us all the pleasant part of England was at an end'. He saw nothing to admire in bracken covered slopes and high crags: they were simply

The River Caldew has its origins in the streams that flow down from Skiddaw, tumbling and dashing through the rock-strewn moorland.

The hill farmers of the Langdales earn their living from the sheep that graze the high fell.

'frightful mountains' to be avoided. What he admired was rich, agricultural land, the flatter the better. Most of his contemporaries shared his views. Then, later in the century, William Gilpin laid out a whole new set of rules for judging scenery, best summed up in one question: is it picturesque? Gilpin knew just what he meant by picturesque – literally: would the scene look good in a picture, and not just any picture, but the sort of romantic landscapes popularised by Poussin and Claude.

Now the shattered crag was more highly regarded than the fertile plain: the blasted oak more handsome than an entire orchard of productive trees – and travel writers soon realised that the Lake District was as picturesque as anywhere in Britain. Dr John Brown's description of a scene near Keswick is typical of the overblown exaggeration of many of his contemporaries.

Once the latest thing in technology, an old hand-cranked chaff-cutting machine rusts beside a Lakeland barn.

You will find rocks and cliffs of stupendous height, hanging over the lake in horrible grandeur, the woods climbing up their steep and shaggy sides, where mortal foot never yet approached; on those dreadful heights the eagles build their nests: a variety of waterfalls are seen pouring from their summits, and tumbling in vast sheets from rock to rock in rude and terrible magnificence: while on all sides of this immense amphitheatre the lofty mountains rise round, piercing the clouds in shapes as spiry and fantastic as the very rocks of Dovedale.

The tourists who came to the region were not at first quite sure exactly which ruins they were supposed to admire and set down for posterity in polite watercolours. West's *Guide to the Lakes* made all plain. 'Stations' were numbered, and precise directions given on how to reach the perfect viewpoint. At Coniston, for example, the amateur artist was directed past a yew tree, through a gate and over a bridge to just one particular 'fragment of dark coloured rock', and there and nowhere else was the easel to be set up for the 'correct' view.

Soon, however, the tourists who came to stare at the picturesque scenes from afar, began to feel that they might enjoy a closer acquaintance. Mrs Radcliffe, who, at the time, was famous as a writer of Gothic novels full of unmentionable terrors, was quite prepared to submit to the genuine excitement of a trip to the summit of Skiddaw on horseback. She could scarcely bear to look at the mountain streams 'hurrying into the abyss' and when she came out on the ridge, she declared it to be 'dreadfully sublime' and so terrifying as to reduce the whole party to silence. So, while we think of Wordsworth and the Lake Poets as starting the rush of tourists to the Lakes, the whole idea of the picturesque was developed while he was still a child. What the travel writers of the mid-eighteenth century began, he elaborated and refined. The popularity of the region grew until, with the arrival of the railway age in the next century, everyone could reach the area. The Lakes had a place of honour on the tourist map.

The old Coniston Hall stands at the point where the Way turns inland from the lakeside

THE
CUMBRIA
WAY

1 ULVERSTON TO CONISTON

via Broughton Beck and Gawthwaite   *14½ miles (23 km)*

The walk starts in the old market town of Ulverston, which first received its charter in the thirteenth century. It has considerable charm, with its old cobbled streets and associations with two famous men of very different achievements. There is a memorial in the church – itself an interesting building of Norman origin – to Sir John Barrow, the Arctic explorer. He is commemorated in even grander style by a monument in the form of a lighthouse that stands on Hoad Hill **A**. The second celebrity is Stan Laurel, who was born in the town and whose life is celebrated in the Laurel and Hardy Museum, housed not in his modest birthplace but in the home of one of his most avid admirers, who put the collection together.

To reach the start of the walk from the town centre follow the signs to the Glass Blowing Museum. The Museum itself is part of Heron Glassworks at the edge of a large car park. Cross the car park to a footpath sign, pointing up to a lane beside a beck. This is the official start of the Cumbria Way **1**. The town is quickly left behind for a pleasant walk beside the busy stream, where the opposite bank rises steeply as a wooded slope with angular rock outcrops over which noisy rooks wheel and quarrel. Where the woodland ends to the left, turn left **2** onto the path between stone walls. It crosses the beck and then climbs steeply up past the end of the wood. Go through a kissing gate, and just before reaching the road, turn right through a squeeze stile onto a path signposted to Old Hall Farm. Continue up the field with the wall on the left to reach a stile beside a gate. Beyond that the view opens up to a gentle countryside of fields spread over rolling hills with Hoad Hill and its lightless lighthouse over to the right. The path goes round to the left of a prominent hill where it joins a track that leads on to Old Hall Farm, which enjoys a delightful situation with shapely Flan Hill to one side and woodland creeping down the hillside to the west.

At the farm **3,** take the stile by the gate on the right to go into the farmyard. Immediately beyond the house turn left through a stile to take the path beside the beck for a few yards. Once past the end of the house, cross the stone stile on the left and head diagonally across the field to a squeeze stile at the side of the wood. Continue on the path beside the dense wood of mainly beech and birch, and a steep little

climb – a modest limbering up for what lies ahead – leads to a wooden stile and a first distant view across to the Lakeland fells. Once across the stile, turn right to follow the path beside the fence and there is a fine view back, looking down over Old Hall Farm to Morecambe Bay. The path now swings round to the left, still going slightly uphill to pass in front of the imposing house. The path swings to follow the line of a little stream to pass the house on the left. Cross a wooden stile and carry straight on, over a farm track, to continue uphill by the stream. This part of the route is waymarked by yellow arrows. Where the woods end on the right, turn right to cross the beck by a stone wall and, after crossing a stone stile, continue straight on towards a ladder stile by a patch of gorse. Take the obvious path through the bushes. The Way continues over a little rocky knoll and then heads down a slight depression to turn left over a stile in the wall on the left. It is well worth going a few steps beyond this turn, however, to reach the top of the rise for a magnificent view out over Ulverston and Morecambe Bay **B**. The path now leads on to Higher Lath Farm **4**.

The Hoad monument, built to commemorate Sir John Barrow, the Arctic explorer, looks out over Morecambe Bay.

Turn right down the road, which twists downhill towards a complex patchwork of fields. Just before the next farm **5,** turn sharp left on the path – one of the few turnings on the whole route actually signposted for the Cumbria Way – and go through the metal gate to take the path with the stone wall to the right. Go through the farmyard with some magnificent slate-roofed stone barns and continue down the surfaced road. When this farm road begins to swing round to the right, carry straight on through the metal gate into the field, and walk ahead with the wall on the right to a metal gate opposite. A set of wind generators comes into view up ahead. At the stone stile by a wooden gate, continue across the field in the direction of the farm. A stile can soon be seen just beyond the telegraph pole. Cross this and the stream and head across the field to the wooden gate in front of the house. Carry straight on, leaving the buildings to your right to pass a telegraph pole with a yellow arrow as a waymark to reach a little gate and the path leading onto the next farm. Where the wall gives way to a wire fence, turn right through a gate and continue in the same direction following the line of a little beck. Go through the iron gate to the left of the house and turn right through the farmyard to take the farm road to the right.

At the road **6**, turn left. There is a wide prospect over a landscape of neat green fields, but now rougher, darker moorland can be seen beyond them and higher hills rise in the distance. The route now follows this quiet country lane, with tempting blackberries beside the way in late summer. Where the road begins to turn left **7**, turn right onto the footpath, signposted to St John's Church. The obvious path across the fields leads to the little church, which with its slate walls and roof and tiny steeple sits comfortably at home in its surroundings **C**. Join the road at the church and turn right, then left along the main road, signposted to Broughton. At the next road junction, turn right to Broughton Beck. Where the road turns right **8**, carry straight on along the road marked as a dead end. Where the way divides by a post with two yellow arrows, turn left on the broad track that runs down to a beck. Do not cross the stone slab bridge, but turn left through the metal gate and head up towards the wind farm on the horizon.

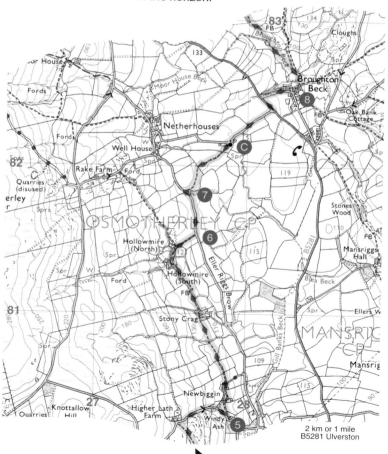

2 km or 1 mile
B5281 Ulverston

As the walls begin to close in, look out for a stone stile on the right. Once over it, turn away from the wall towards the middle of the field to cross a simple stone slab bridge across the beck. Turn left to take a path over a series of small stiles alongside the beck, shaded by alder and blackthorn. Beck and path part company, the latter continuing on a straight line with a stone wall on the left and the crumbling remains of another wall to the right. Soon the next objective, Knapperthaw Farm, comes into view. The path bends round the bottom of a steep-sided hill covered in gorse to join the road **9**.

Turn left on the road past the farm, then turn right at the next road junction, where the view opens out over the rough moorland of Lowick Common. At the next T-junction **10**, turn left and, after 30 paces, turn right onto a metalled track and over a cattle grid. The track bends right through a gateway, immediately beyond which is a footpath sign by a clump of trees. Turn left to cross first a ladder stile and then a plain stile, then turn right to pass behind the house, heading for a stone stile in the corner of the field. Turn slightly left on a diagonal across the field to a narrow stile. Carry on with the stone wall to the left, passing a creep hole used by sheep who have created their very own path through the wall. The track now runs between stone walls to the farm, and passes through the yard via two gates to arrive at the road and the village of

The Way near Gawthwaite, meandering beside the stone walls that separate the valley fields from the rougher ground of the fells.

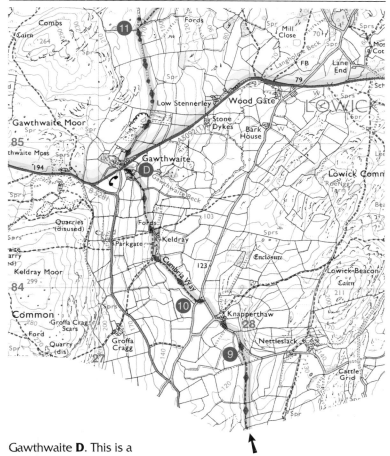

Gawthwaite **D**. This is a
significant point along the Way, for it has now reached the southern
border of the Lake District National Park, and, as one might expect, its
character soon begins to change.

Cross straight over the road to take the road opposite, which turns
right through an attractive group of typical Lakeland cottages then turn
left onto the metalled road going uphill. As the road climbs, there is a
view back to the Hoad Hill monument and all the way across
Morecambe Bay to the squat, square bulk of the nuclear power station at
Heysham. Looking ahead, however, the dominant features are the fells
and the more attractive focal point of the Old Man of Coniston, and there
is just a glimpse of Coniston Water. Soon the surfaced track gives way to
a rougher farm track, then, where a strip of trees comes up to join this
track on the right, turn right through a gate marked 'Footpath Only' **11**.

Looking back over the start of the Cumbria Way from a rocky eminence near Gawthwai

The first of the lakes to be met along the way: a distant prospect of the snow-capped Langdale hills.

A hairpin bend leads down to High Stennerley. Go through the gate to go right round the buildings, following a road that now goes steadily downhill with woodland on the right. At the road, turn right, then immediately left through a metal gate signposted to the Cumbria Way. The ground beyond is something of a marshy quagmire, made worse by being churned up by cattle, and walkers must make their way as best they can to go round to the right of the hillock. Here is another gate and another morass. Pass the next hummock on the right and head for a prominent stone stile by a large oak tree. Continue down to the road **12** and turn left. This is a quiet country road that runs through a knobbly landscape of stony humps, interspersed with patches of woodland and gorse.

Where the road turns sharp right **13**, continue straight on along the bridleway signposted to Kiln Bank. At the farm, turn right immediately beyond the house and follow the track beside the barns. Go through a gate and follow the path round to the left beneath the stone strewn hill-side. Where the way divides by a post with two arrows, take the path on the right running uphill away from the wall. Topping the rise, the next objective comes into view, a whitewashed farmhouse. A ladder stile on the right gives access to an obvious grassy path through bracken and gorse that winds its way up to the farm. This eventually joins into the farm approach road. Where this road levels out, look out for a broad grassy track that leads away to the right, signposted as a public footpath **14**. This is a wholly delightful section, walking on good springy turf above the beautiful Crake Valley. Stone walls meander out from the pasture to climb the bracken slopes to a thick topping of woodland. Beyond the valley, the hills rise up promising more rugged scenery to come – a promise shortly to be fulfilled.

The path now drops down towards the house of Cockenskell. At the bottom of the slope where the track begins to swing left, turn right through a wooden gate with a Cumbria Way sign. The route continues as a track between stone walls. Go through the gate at the end of this section and turn left to take the narrow path heading down the hill, then turn left to cross the beck on a little stone bridge and continue up the path. Where the path immediately divides, take the path to the left beside the fence, which soon becomes a narrow, rough way between the wall and the bracken covered hill. The path then swings away from the wall to head directly up hill, a rough route through bracken and heather and a good stiff climb. At the top of the rise, where the paths cross, continue straight on to Beacon Tarn **E**. This may not be one of the great lakes, but it enjoys a wonderfully remote and wild setting, and is far enough away from roads to be kept peaceful.

The Way goes round the left-hand-side of the tarn. An extra embellishment to the beauty of the scene is found at the northern end of the tarn, where water lilies float on the quiet, dark waters.

The path now heads for the obvious gap between the hills, a good clear path through the bracken. Soon the little col is topped and there is the first really clear view of the Old Man himself. This is all excellent walking with a track that winds down the valley below the craggy hillside to the right and a large area of flat marshland to the left. The path emerges at Stable Harvey Moss strewn with the humps of material left behind by a long-departed glacier. Reaching the lower level, the ground becomes boggy and the path indistinct. The route turns right towards the road, which has now appeared, crosses a stream and climbs up an area of high ground to head for a footpath sign **15**. Turn left onto the road, and after about 50 paces, turn left again onto a track by a second signpost. The broad track soon divides.

Take the right-hand fork heading uphill, which soon swings round to follow the direction of the power lines towards a small, now dis-used, reservoir. The track then swings left and a gurgling beck is heard and then seen. Turn right by the power lines to cross the beck and take the path through the bracken. Where this again divides, take the path on the right down the valley with a shapely hill to the left of it. Cross another small stream and continue along the valley path with the track down below on the right. The trees that appear directly ahead are actually on the far side of Coniston Water. A footbridge now carries the Way over the busy Torver Beck **F**, here at its most dashing as it plunges over a series of rock ledges.

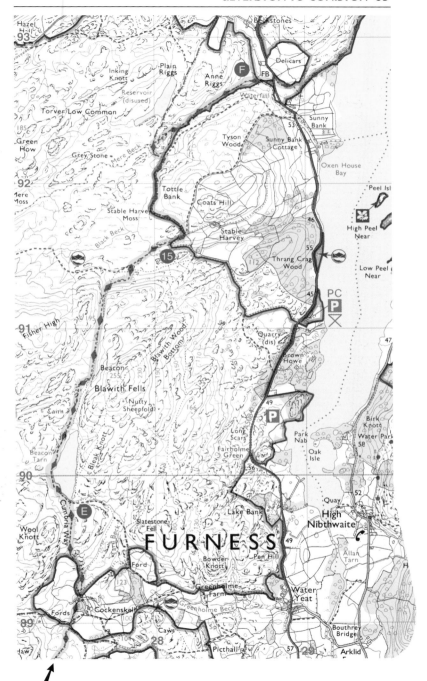

A simple footbridge that helps the walker across one of the many streams on the

moorland below Beacon Tarn.

The boggy ground of Stable Harvey Moss.

The path now leads up to the road **16**. Cross the road and turn right on the path signposted to the lake shore, and almost at once, topping a rise, the lake does indeed come into view. This is a typical glacial lake – long, thin and deep, with steep wooded banks. Go through a kissing gate, and take the obvious grassy path that leads steadily down to the tree-fringed lake, where tall copper beech add a spectacular touch of colour. On reaching the water's edge, turn left and the complications of route finding are over for a good many miles to come. It is not a straight, level path – it bends and twists through the trees, undulates with the terrain – but for two miles it stays close to the water's edge. At first the trees are sparse clumps of mainly birch and oak, but soon the Way passes into a more extensive area of what is at first all broad-leaved woodland, but which soon contains liberal spatterings of conifer. Crossing a narrow stream, the path emerges by the Torver Jetty **G**, a stopping place for the Coniston passenger launch which provides a regular service on the lake and a temptation to cheat on a miserable day! It also provides a way of visiting Brantwood, John Ruskin's home on the far shore of the lake. The Coniston launch boats are elegant craft dating back to the 1920s, but they cannot compete with the steam yacht *Gondola*. She was launched on the lake in 1859 and worked on until 1937 when she was converted into a houseboat and began gradually to deteriorate. Then, in 1977, the beautiful old vessel was restored by the National Trust, and now she steams again on Coniston Water, flying her proud white banner of smoke. A delight to those who travel on board, but almost as great a treat for the walker who sees her out on the water.

Conifers give way again to broad-leaved woodland, dominated by oak, before another clearing appears with a jetty and moorings for a number of boats. This was once the site of an ironworks using local timber to provide charcoal for the furnace but scarcely a trace remains, and tents from the local camp site have replaced the industrial buildings. Woodland is now left behind and there are clear views out over the lake, where excited gulls wheel and scramble over
snootily unimpressed grebe.

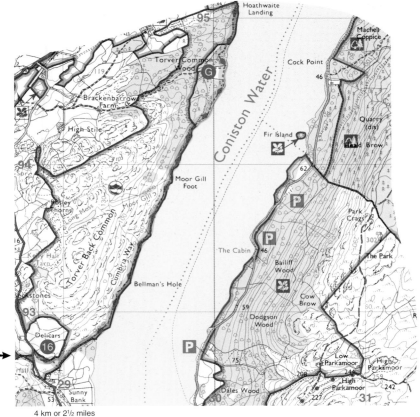

4 km or 2½ miles
A5084 Blawith

Looking north up Coniston Water, with a distant prospect of the snow-capped

Langdale hills.

Where the way ahead is blocked by a stone wall **17**, turn left towards the camp site and follow the track round a copse to join the surfaced road from the site. This heads off towards Coniston Hall **H** with its immense, stepped chimneys and somewhat brooding presence. Follow the road past the Hall, go through the gate at the far side of the grounds and turn right across the grass to a second gate. The path now wings away towards Coniston with its magnificent mountain backdrop. Where the broad path turns sharp right **18**, turn left towards a gate by a prominent clump of trees then right to cross a ladder stile and continue on to a stile by a gate that leads on to the

Boats at the northern end of Coniston Water, close by the Cumbria Way at Coniston Hall.

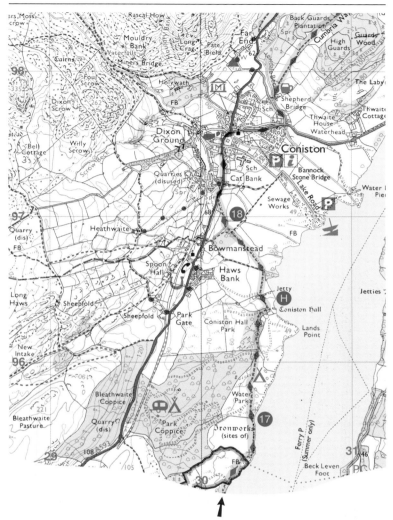

road. Turn right into Coniston. As mentioned, the village is associated with the romantic Victorians, notably John Ruskin, whose memorial in the churchyard combines Gothic and Celtic motifs and whose life and work is celebrated in the nearby museum. The village, however, owes its existence to more mundane matters, as it has been a centre for mining for copper ore and slate over many centuries. An attractive spot to pause, with its mountain stream bustling through the centre of the village, it is also the starting point for those who wish to climb to the 803 metre (2635 ft) summit of the Old Man mountain.

Traditional lakeland cottage near Tarn Hows, using local slate for both walls and roofs.

Ascent of The Old Man of Coniston

6 miles (10 km)

The route leaves Coniston via Station Hill, passing the former Furness Railway Station **A**, closed in the Beeching cuts of 1958. One feature that remains is the old slate loading wharf. Continue on the surfaced road to Fell Gate **B**. Just before the car park, turn right up the rough track, originally used for bringing slate down from the Old Man Quarries. The slope is quite gentle at first, and remains of former slate mines and quarries can be seen on the slope to the left. Where a track

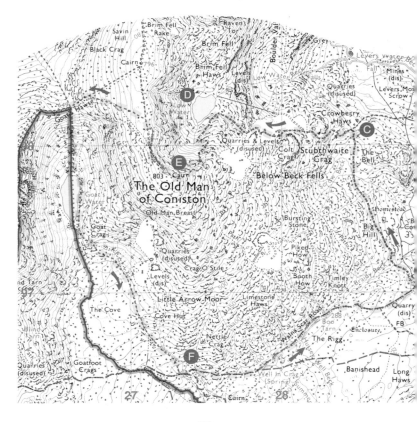

comes up the hill from the right from Coppermines Valley, which was just what its name suggests **C,** the route turns left through a complex of old slate workings and begins to climb more steeply. Soon Low Water Tarn **D,** which in certain weather conditions can appear a startlingly bright blue due to copper in the underlying rocks, comes into view. Here the track turns left to climb out of the end of the small combe holding the tarn, and begins to zig-zag left then right before climbing steeply up the shoulder to the summit cairn **E** at the height of over 2500 feet (750 metres).

From here, turn right for an exhilarating walk along the summit ridge to an obvious track that looks down over a steep rocky slope to reach a junction of paths at Goat's Hawse, with the rock faces of Dow Crag rising above the combe. Turn left to take the track down to Goat's Water, which turns along the left bank of the tarn. This very clear path runs down to Walna Scar Road, an even more obvious track **F**. Turn left here and, where the way divides, take the clear route to the right to return to Fell Gate and the road back to Keswick.

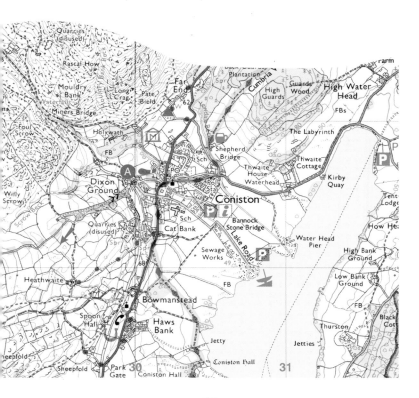

2 Coniston to Dungeon Ghyll

via Skelwith Bridge and Elterwater   *11 miles (17.5 km)*

Take the road past the church and continue on the road to the right of the Crown Hotel. At the next road junction just before the bridge **19**, turn left down the road signposted to Ambleside. Continue past the football ground, then turn right opposite the school to cross the beck on a stone bridge. Turn immediately left over a stone stile and continue through a gate to take the path beside the beck. This is an area of National Trust land where the old meadows are being conserved. The path follows the line of a wall, the way shaded by some sturdy old oaks. Passing the ruins of what was once an ornate barn with Gothic arches, the Way now heads uphill beside the fence on the right. The well-defined path reaches a line of conifers, and it is worth pausing to look back and enjoy the view over the lake. Then, as the path winds up through gorse, take a glance at the wall on the left. It is typical of the area, made up of stone cleared from the land with massive boulders at its base. The path goes over a stile to dip into woodland and past an impressively spreading yew to a gate. Beyond this the Way levels out to go through an area of mixed woodland.

Leaving the wood, the Way follows an old track with evidence of stone surfacing. Here there are immense views out to the left of the crags of Yewdale Fells with streams pouring down the flank like white lines trailed by an erratic paint brush, while in the distance there are views on to the even more impressive hills of the Langdales. The path keeps close to the wall on the left, and, where the wall comes to an end, turns half-left. This section of the route is waymarked by yellow arrows. Once past a large oak, head for the gate in the wall and continue on to a stile next to the gate by the prominent group of trees **20**. Turn left onto the wide, stony track signposted to Tarn Hows. It arrives back at Yewdale Beck, running deep and clear, and the stream is followed to a handsome stone bridge, with its parapet turned to end in neat columns **A**. Do not cross the bridge, but continue up beside the water heading towards the woods. Leave the fields by a stile to enter the woodland and continue on the very obvious path beside the beck. Soon, however, the path swings away to begin a steady climb and the way becomes narrower and rougher. Cross a footbridge to enter even denser woodland, where oak rear up above

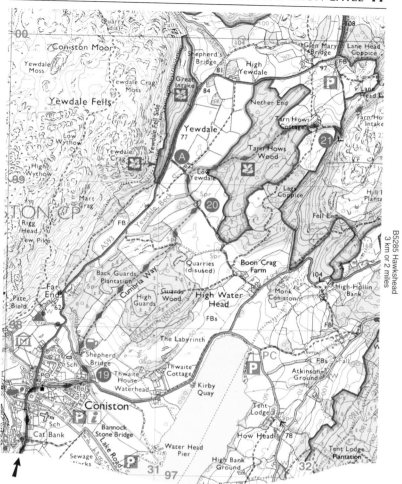

young birch and alder, the spaces in between filled with dense clumps of fern. Cross an unusual gated stile which brings another change, this time to conifers, before a second gated stile leads back to broad-leaved woodland. The path still climbs, but now, nearing the edge of the wood, the views open on a deep wooded valley surrounded by crags. Tarn Hows cottage appears marking the edge of the woodland. Go through the gate by the magnificent horse chestnut to pass this delightful house with its very enviable view. At the cottage approach road **21**, turn right and the drive immediately swings away sharply to the left, with a view down to Yew Tree Tarn

Tarn Hows: a spot which owes its popularity as much to its setting high in the hills as to its intrinsic beauty.

and its encircling trees. Turn left at the road, and the view changes once again. Looking over to the left, there is the long ridge of the Yewdale Fells, bubbling with rocks and topped by the spiky silhouettes of pine, as if in a Japanese painting. Beyond this the higher peaks, including Scafell, can be seen. The road leads on to a car park and the path now continues straight on to Tarn Hows **B**. This is one of the most famous, and popular, beauty spots in the region, known for its attractive setting among the hills and also for the majestic native pine that surround it and bristle from the island. It seems the perfect example of natural beauty, but is in fact artificial – created by damming a stream to serve an old watermill.

The route follows the well-trodden path up the left of the tarn. There is a complex network of paths through the woods, but the Way follows the route closest to the water's edge round to the far end of the lake.

Carry straight on along the footpath signposted to Arnside and the Langdales. Cross a ladder stile **22** and turn left on the path to the Langdales, passing a little round tarn at the edge of the woods. The Way now follows a broad track running between stone walls through typical Lakeland scenery. On the valley floor are the fields for pasture, above them the rougher slopes of bracken and trees and beyond them all a more distant prospect of high hills. There are constant small variations in the view as the path dips and turns, before continuing downhill on a surfaced track. Cross straight over the busy main road **23** and immediately turn right to take the footpath at the edge of the woods. Leave the woods by a ladder stile and continue beside the wall which cuts off the sight if not the sound of traffic. Cross another ladder stile at the start of the woodland and continue along the wall but now on the opposite side.

A593 Coniston
2 km or 1 mile

The waterfall of Skelwith Force, a popular site close to the road at Skelwith Bridge.

At the road junction **24**, turn left onto the minor road, which begins by heading downhill, but is soon switchbacking furiously with the wood to one side and a boulder strewn field to the other. Eventually it heads down towards High Park farm. Just before reaching the house **25**, turn right through a kissing gate onto the footpath waymarked by a blue arrow which heads straight for the woodland. Once inside the wood, the way divides, offering a choice of routes. That to the right is the more direct, but the path to the left offers a far more interesting route and is definitely recommended. It is this route which is now described. Take the path, signposted to Colwith Force, that plunges downhill and swings right by a massive beech with widespread branches. The path becomes narrower and smoother and soon the river comes into view, rushing and swirling round a tight bend. Follow the riverside path past a series of small waterfalls until the Force itself **C** suddenly comes dramatically into sight. It seems extraordinary that these immense falls are not better known, but their wild situation makes their appearance all the more exciting. The path now continues beside the still-busy river to the road **26** where the two routes reunite. Turn right at the road, cross a beck and turn left over a stile to take the path signposted to Skelwith Bridge. There is a short but steep climb up the river bank, and from there an obvious path leads towards a house. Go through an iron gate and straight over the driveway to a stile to continue on the footpath, which soon becomes a little lane running between hedges through farmland, with clusters of houses down on the road. Take the path straight on between the farm buildings, which heads downhill towards Skelwith Bridge. The path passes Park House by a pair of kissing gates. Where the track divides, with the road in view on the right, turn left down a rougher path which leads briefly into a patch of woodland before reaching the road **27**.

Turn left on the road to Skelwith Bridge and cross the bridge. Once over, turn immediately sharp left as indicated by the footpath signposted to Elterwater. The path heads for the Kirkstone Galleries, where the local green slate is processed in their workshops and sold and displayed in their show-room. Go past the workshops to join the riverside walk. A number of footbridges provide viewing galleries to see Skelwith Force, where a natural fault has created a 16-foot (5-metre) drop over which the River Brathay plunges – a fine sight but, it has to be said, not as spectacular as Colwith Force. After the drama, things become a good deal calmer. Beyond the falls, a wooden gate gives access to grassy fields and the path heads across them to the left of a prominent clump of trees. The river has now become calmer and gradually widens until, almost imperceptibly, it becomes the lake of Elter

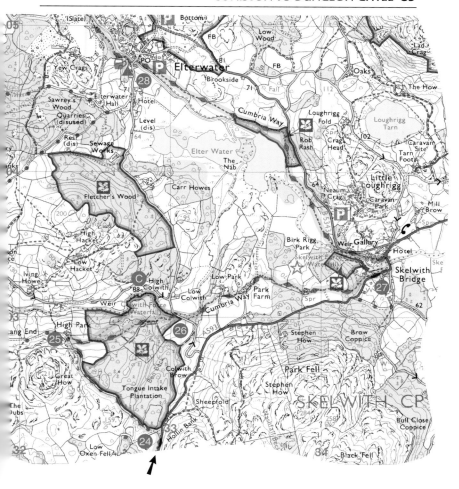

Water. The rugged landscape is temporarily left behind as swans glide on the lake, cows chew their way across the fields which, with their scattering of mature trees, seem more like parkland. But there is a promise of the return to wildness as the Langdale Pikes rise up ahead. There is an excursion into woodland for a way before the path joins the river to head off towards the village of Elterwater.

At the edge of the village many might like to turn to the right to visit this most attractive spot with houses and pub grouped round a green. To continue on the Way, however, turn left over the bridge **28** and then immediately right up the quarry road passing great mounds of slate spoil. New housing across the river, built of local materials, sits coyly

Stake Pass can be a daunting spot in winter when ice piles up in the streams and coa

...e rocks in white.

behind a screen of trees. The cavernous opening of an old slate quarry is passed on the left and now the footpath turns back towards the river, darting merrily along over rocky ledges. The Way threads a path between the river and the spoil heaps to a wooden footbridge **29**. Cross over and turn left on the road by Wainwrights Inn – named after waggon builders, not the famous Lakeland fell walker. Turn left off the road onto the footpath which swings round the back of Chapel Stile. The little church sits stubbornly four-square beneath shattered crags and the levels of old slate workings. The track leads past Thrang Farm and then runs between stone walls, passing mountains of spoil held back behind high retaining walls. Cross the river by a shapely low-arched bridge **30** and turn right up the riverside path into Great Langdale.

This is a typically high-sided glacial valley of impressive crags interlaced with the white threads of hill streams. Now the path leaves the

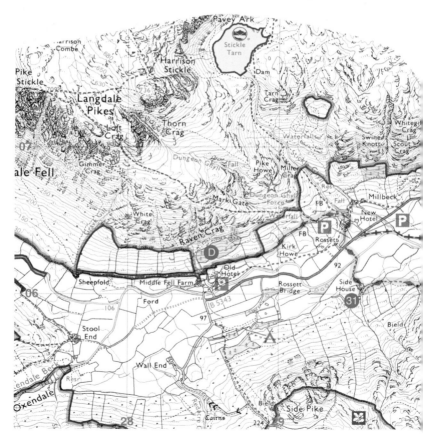

river to Oak Howe, where it swings round behind the barns to take a rough, stony route round the foot of the hillside. Across the valley, a prominent streak of water marks the stream that pours out of Stickle Tarn high among the Langdale Pikes and cascades down the deep gully of Dungeon Ghyll. Up ahead, the valley can be seen to close in, promising hard work in the near future. This section ends at a wooden gate, after which the way heads downhill across the fields on a cobbled path. Cross the beck at a wooden footbridge by the farm buildings **31** and take the farm approach road to head down to the main road up the valley. Turn left and then immediately right to enter the National Trust car park. Carry on through to take the path signposted to Stickle Tarn and go between two plantations of young trees to head up towards the New Dungeon Ghyll Hotel. Here a gate on the left gives access to a fellside path just above the level of the wall. The Way continues on the obvious route up the valley, with road and river down below and the steep face of Raven Crag, a popular place for rock climbers, up above the scree to the right. It continues on to the Old Dungeon Ghyll Hotel **D**, a favourite stopping place for walkers and climbers for many generations, and here the road doubles back to head through the hills to Little Langdale, leaving the way ahead to the walker.

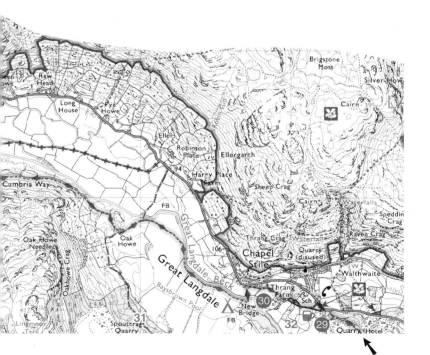

3 DUNGEON GHYLL TO KESWICK

via Stake Pass and Rosthwaite • *15½ miles (25 km)*

The Way continues on the obvious rough track just above the level of the valley floor, signposted to Mickleden. There is a true grandeur to the scene. The beck waters the valley floor which seems almost unnaturally green when seen against the sombre grey of the crags. The very end of the valley is Y-shaped as two streams pour down either side of a great rocky bluff that occupies the middle ground, with Bowfell to the south and the Pikes spilling their scree down the

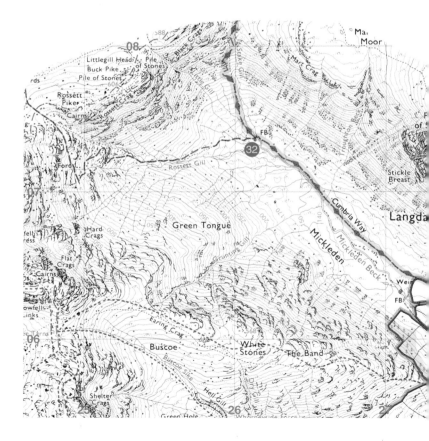

slopes to the north. A solitary farm huddles up at the valley end **A**, as the path begins to swing north to take the right-hand branch of the Y and head towards the daunting Stake Pass. All the time now the scenery is getting wilder, although the going remains easy, staying close to the valley floor. But at the same time, the hills are closing in, with the shapely stone peak of Pike of Stickle looming above the Way. Streams course down the hill, mostly carried across the path in neat culverts: this is a popular route and to avoid erosion is kept regularly covered in loose stone. Walkers should keep to the recognised way to help protect this unique environment.

Cross over a footbridge **32** and then, where the way divides by a sheepfold, leave the more obvious track and turn right up the narrower track that climbs up beside the dashing beck, zig-zagging ever more extravagantly as the climb steepens. This is the most severe test of the Cumbria Way, a thousand-foot climb up a rough, steep path, but the effort is more than amply rewarded. The view back down Great Langdale is sensational and one soon begins to see the distant prospects beyond the immediate summits. And there is still more to come. There are delights too, nearer at hand as the beck leaps down through the rocks. The top of the pass represents a quite amazing

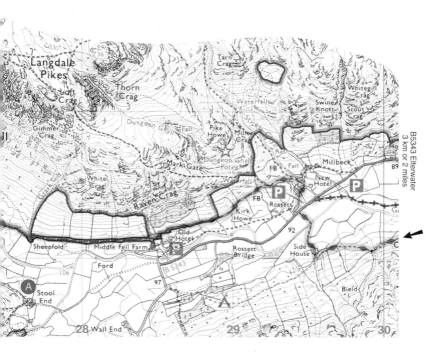

The strange, hummocky landscape through which the Way picks a tortuous path at

...d of the Stake Pass.

A small tarn marks the start of the descent to Borrowdale.

landscape **B** of hummocks, looking more like ancient burial mounds than natural features, interspersed with areas of peaty bog. The clear path continues straight on until it reaches the other side of the combe, and here another breath-stopping landscape unfolds, as you find yourself perched on the rim of the wild, deep valley of Langstrath with the dark bulk of Great Gable over to the west and the prominent outline of Skiddaw up ahead. This is literally a watershed on the walk, for now streams and rivers will flow north instead of south, heading towards the Solway Firth and the Scottish border.

The path heads as steeply downhill as it has climbed up the other side, with Stake Beck burbling alongside for company. Reaching the valley floor, cross the footbridge **33** and continue up the valley. Here, in this wild and lonely spot two streams which have hurtled down the hillsides converge as Langstrath Beck, which the path now follows down the valley. This can be a very silent place with little but the sound of running water, and not much company apart from the occasional bird, perhaps a wheatear waggling its white rump and giving out its harsh little cry. The path is very rough and crossed by a number of small streams, but soon the first stone wall appears, crossed by a ladder stile. Beyond this, the walker has to pick a route through rocks and boulders before a more definite path is established, running beside a wall. After a wooden gate, the path becomes a lot easier as the stony hillside gives way to grassland, and the way joins the river, rushing over a series of falls. Do not cross the footbridge on the left over Langstrath Beck **34** but

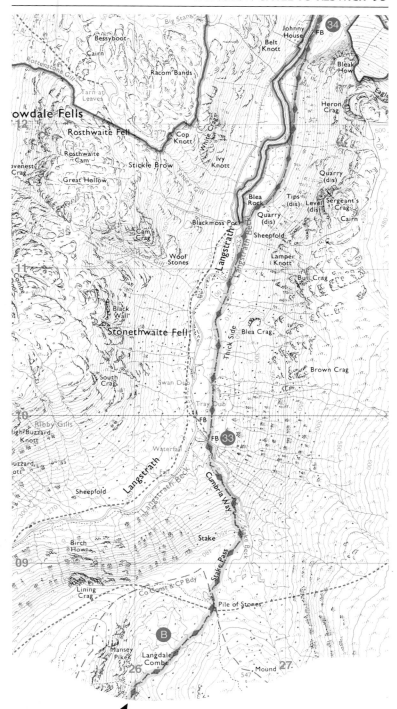

Looking back up the Way from the path beside the busy Langstrath Beck.

The Langstrath Beck has carved a deep gorge for itself in its rapid descent from Bowfell.

continue on the same side. As the beck bends away to the left, go through the wooden gate and stay at the river's edge. Flat rocks by attractive falls **C** make this a tempting place to linger.

A second stream comes down from the hills on the right and is crossed by a footbridge, after which the way turns left up the ever widening valley. It is all very attractive as the river rushes down narrow rock gorges. However, everything soon becomes gentler and houses appear up ahead to mark the entry into Borrowdale. The narrow, rough path gives way to a wide, grassy track and trees soften the hard edge of the hills. A footbridge on the left leads to Stonethwaite, but the Cumbria Way continues along the same bank. This is now very much back to the fertile valley floor with fields divided not just by walls but now by hedgerows, while trees dot the fields. The path wanders briefly away from the river then rejoins it for a tree-shaded walk into Rosthwaite.

Turn left over the bridge **35** and continue to the road, and there turn left and immediately right on the minor road that leads up to Yew Tree Farm with its fine flock of Herdwick sheep. Once through the farm buildings, the path swings right towards the River Derwent. If the water levels are low, the river can be crossed here and followed round to the right; otherwise, continue on the same side to New Bridge **36** with its low arch, where crossing may be easier. Continue beside the river and, after crossing a stile, follow the path that swings away to pass behind a wooded knoll. The route now runs into broad-leaf woodland, full of majestic mature trees, above which grey crags rise up the hillside. The walk passes the cavernous entry to an old slate quarry with its surrounding heaps of spoil **D**.

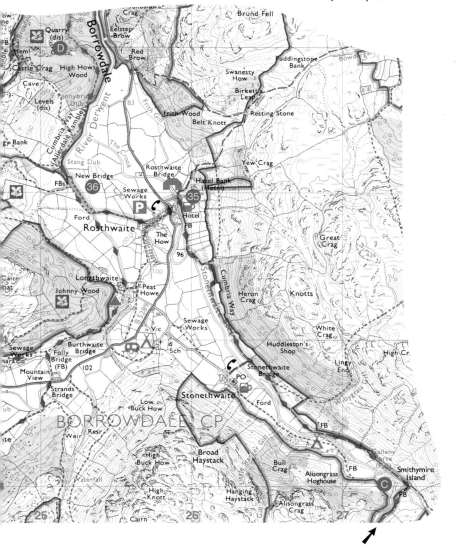

The head of Borrowdale, where the rough, wild fells give way to fields and houses

After a short climb, turn right at a junction of tracks, go downhill to a gap in the wall, beyond which a rough, stony track leads steeply downhill. At the bottom, it gives way to a broader track which returns to the river, now flowing placidly. Where it runs round a gravel island, turn away from the river to join the approach road to the camp site **37**.

Turn left at the track, which goes through Hollows farmyard. The way continues as a rough track, with the village of Grange in the bottom of the valley, seen against a background of craggy, wooded hills with just a first glint of Derwent Water in the distance. Where the way ahead is blocked by a wall at the edge of a wood, go through the wooden gate in the wall on the right **38**. Head across the field on the path that curves round a solitary holly tree, and head downhill towards the road. At the roadway, turn left and, after crossing a stream, turn right onto a track signposted Public Footpath to Lodore **39**. Cross the plank bridge over the stream and go through a kissing gate to take the path round the outside of the wood, and at the edge of the wood take the path on the left down to the lake shore.

Plank walkways now lead round to a path up the western side of the lake. It is worth pausing at this point to enjoy the magnificent view back

New Bridge, an old cobbled packhorse bridge that crosses that River Derwent near Rosthwaite.

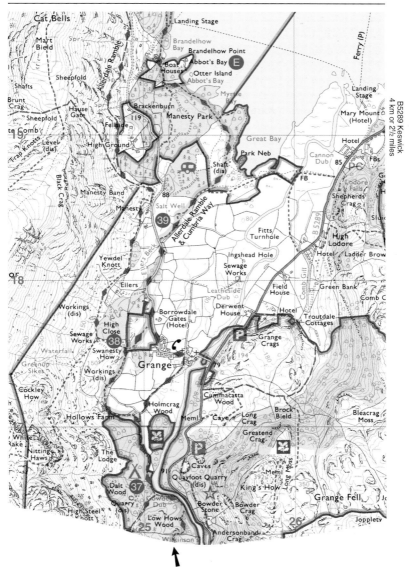

B5289 Keswick
4 km or 2½ miles

up Borrowdale. The lakeside walk is very popular with visitors and is
easy to follow with gravel paths and bridges across the becks. It runs
through mixed woodland, sometimes heading into the trees, at other
times meeting the water at little inlets. The Way briefly joins a surfaced
road that leads down to Abbot's Bay, an enchanting spot with its jetty
and moored boats and a clear view across the lake **E**. There are many

tracks through the woods, but the Way stays on those paths closest to the lake, with easy going all the way, and a chance to catch sight of the Keswick Launch, giving visitors a different view of Derwent Water. An islet comes into view humped and spiked with trees like a giant pin cushion. Leave the wood by a gate **40** and turn left away from the lake, past a clearing studded with magnificent trees, including an aged spreading oak. Turn right on the surfaced track signposted to Keswick.

At the road **41**, turn right, and then at the road junction, turn right, not down the surfaced track, but on the footpath that leads into the woods. The path goes steeply downhill, crossing a clearing, and heads back into the woods on the far side. The walk takes on a quite different character, closely confined by dense, overgrown thickets. It runs past an area of rhododendra and conifers, before the trees clear rather unexpectedly to reveal a large house. This is Lingholm **F**, noted for its formal and woodland gardens, seen at their best when the azaleas and rhododendra are in bloom. Cross straight over the driveway and continue on the track beside the wall. Where the way divides **42**, continue straight forward on the narrower path through the trees, where tall beech hang their branches over the way. At the road **43**, turn right. At the road junction **44**, do not follow the road to the left signposted to Keswick, but take the minor road to the right. The road ends and is continued as a footpath that leads to an alarmingly noisy suspension bridge. Once over the bridge, turn right through a gateway that leads to a path across the fields. Where a fence nears the path on the right, there is a footpath up to the main road, to continue on the Way **45**, but most walkers will want to continue straight on to visit Keswick, for accommodation, refreshment or simply to contemplate just how much money they could spend in the plethora of specialist shops selling walking and climbing gear. To reach the town centre, turn right at the main road.

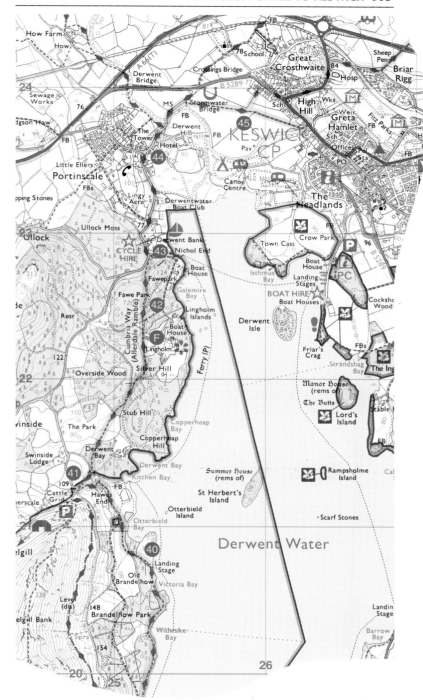

4 KESWICK TO CALDBECK

Eastern Route via High Peak   *14 miles (22 km)*
Western Route via Whitewater Dash   *16½ miles (26.5 km)*

Those who have turned off at **45** should turn right on the B5289; those who have gone into Keswick should leave on the Cockermouth road. At the road junction **46**, turn up the main Carlisle road and take the first right turn, signposted to Skiddaw. Where the houses end on the left **47**, turn left on to the public bridleway also indicated as the Skiddaw route. A bridge takes the track over the busy main road and climbs up into woodland, a good area to look for red squirrels that can be heard chuntering away among the trees. As the path climbs,

A small bay at the southern end of Derwent Water, with pebble beach and boat house.

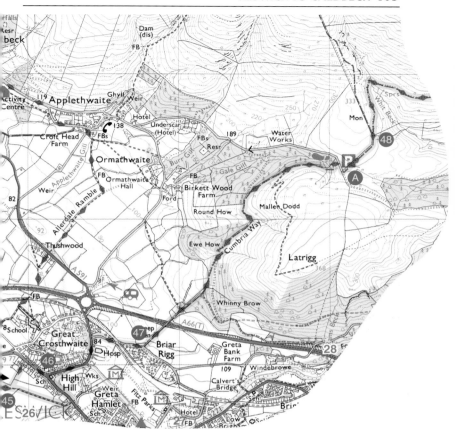

the view opens out over Derwent Water and Bassenthwaite Lake. Where the way divides, keep to the left on the path that goes along the edge of the woods. After a stiff climb, the path levels out to contour the hill, following the edge of a dense conifer plantation. The path eventually arrives at a car park **A**, a magnificent viewpoint and the starting place for the ascent of Skiddaw.

To continue on the Cumbria Way take the narrow path between wall and fence at the end of the car park. It turns out onto open moorland where the Way divides **48**, the left-hand path leading up Skiddaw and the Way following the path to the right, which leads off to the head of a deep ghyll with a vast expanse of wild fells opening up to the north. This section of the walk lies at the very edge of the Lake District, with a view out to the east of a quite different, greener countryside. This is all

Skiddaw House hostel with Skiddaw in the background. Here the Cumbria Way divides, and the western route can be clearly seen.

excellent walking on a grassy track high up the hillside with long vistas and the occasional buzzard mewing overhead. The track rounds the end of the ghyll and begins to swing left to head up another dramatic valley. At first the path is narrow and stony, clinging to a narrow ledge beneath the Lonscale Crags. The hills across the ghyll and in sight up ahead now have a different character, more rounded with patches of bracken and heather and trickles of scree. As the path nears the head of the valley, the rocks are left behind for wide expanses of grassy moorland. Then a stile is crossed and the Way heads for a footbridge over a wide stream before climbing up a heather-covered hillside to the clump of trees that shield Skiddaw Youth Hostel **49**.

A choice now has to be made. The more direct, and in many ways more attractive, route heads off to the wild fells and will climb to an altitude of over 2000 feet (610 metres). Paths are often indistinct and, if clouds are low, route finding will prove difficult. So, if the clouds are already covering the tops in view from the hostel, then it would be wiser to take the alternative route to the west, which has its own drama and delights. The shorter eastern route over High Peak will be described first; the description of the alternative begins on page 114.

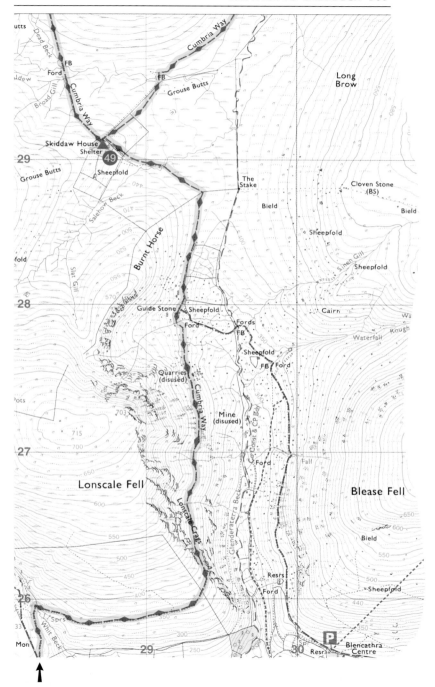

The Eastern Route

Do not follow the obvious wide track leading away from the hostel, but turn right to take the footpath beside the wall. This leads downhill through peaty moorland to cross the beck by a footbridge, and then climbs back up the valley side. This seems one of the loneliest sections of the whole walk with moorland stretching away in every direction. Only the occasional wall and sheep fold suggest that anyone has ever changed the land from its natural state. The path comes close to the beck that writhes and gurgles on its tortuous way, eventually to swell out with its many contributions from hill streams to form the River Caldew, which will be met again further along the Way. The track soon becomes much wider to accommodate the vehicles that bring shooters to the grouse butts which can be seen on the slope to the left. After such a taste of wildness and loneliness, it comes as a surprise, and something of a disappointment, to see a road up ahead – but it will be no more than a minor interruption.

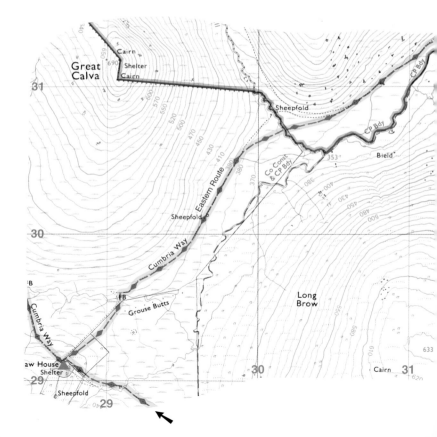

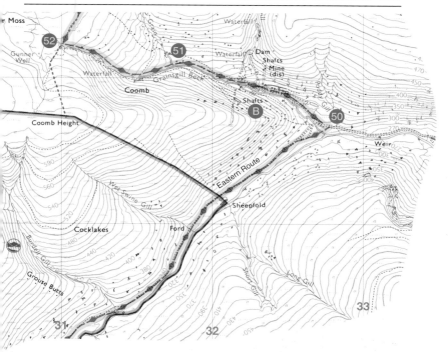

Cross the bridge over the fast-flowing Grainsgill Beck **50** and, at the road, turn left up the track beside the beck. Looking out along the road one can see expansive views over woods and fields towards Penrith. The well-made track runs up towards old surface buildings, shafts and spoil heaps of a former tungsten mine **B**. This is only one of the minerals extracted from these hills: there are lead mines at higher levels and barium to the north. Quartz glints in the rocks near the mine, though the immediate surroundings have an aura of barren desolation. Once past the mine, however, everything changes. The well-made track ends and gives way to a grassy path beside the beck, which becomes less and less distinct the higher up the hill you climb. The most obvious path keeps close to the bounding stream, which is joined by another hill stream, Arm o'Grain **51**. Here it may be necessary to go upstream along this second beck to make an easy crossing. Soon the beck sides begin to close in and walkers have to find their way as best they can while still climbing and keeping close to the beck. A small waterfall provides a welcome indication that the top of this rough, steep ascent is near. Once over the brow of the hill, turn right on the obvious track **52** that heads past a lonely hut.

The busy river Caldew keeps the eastern route company for a while after Skiddaw Hou.

The route has now reached a height of almost 2000 feet (610 metres) and the last of the long, serious climbs is over, providing a chance to enjoy the immense views out over the low-lying land to the east. The path cuts past the summit of Great Lingy Hill rising gently out of the surrounding moorland and across a plateau by a small cairn. Up ahead is the more obvious rise of High Pike. Follow the broad track that swings right, then shortly beyond the turn strike off on the path to the left **53** to reach the summit **C**. This is the highest point on the Cumbria Way and it is not a disappointment. On a clear day – and if it is not a clear day you probably should not be here – there is an immense panorama, which takes in the hills of Scotland beyond the Solway Firth. A memorial seat provides a welcome opportunity to enjoy it all in comfort.

Continue along the summit ridge, looking for the village of Caldbeck, which can be seen below. There is no obvious path, so once again it is up to the individual to find the best route with Caldbeck as the landmark – or, if visibility is poor, then head due north by compass. After descending for a while, a nearer objective becomes clear: a deep ghyll, its sides scarred with mine spoil. Reaching the top of the ghyll **54**, take the track that leads away on an angle to the right and the main objective. Nether Row can be seen – not the large whitewashed farm at the foot of the hill, but the larger group of houses a little to the east of it. A clear, grassy track leads down to the houses **55**. Go straight down the track to join the road, where the two routes reunite.

A stony path through the gorse on the approach to Caldbeck.

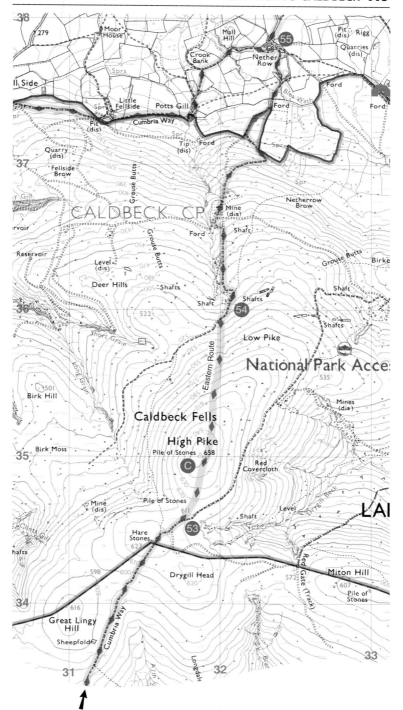

A distant view of Bassenthwaite Lake from the eastern branch of the Way.

THE WESTERN ROUTE

From the gates of the youth hostel, take the obvious, broad track that heads off across heather moorland. A small stream is crossed by the ford or footbridge, after which the track climbs steadily past bogs, where emerald green patches of moss stand out among the heather. The track begins to swing left and a gap in the hills up ahead reveals that the fells are giving way to farmland. There is a steady descent and now a beck comes into view on the left. The Way now twists down to cross the stream, which burbles over small falls to the left, but plunges over the edge at the appropriately named Whitewater Dash to the right **D**. The track continues to head downhill past Dead Crags, more ominous in name than in appearance, and now looking back there is a much better view of the high falls. Down in the valley,

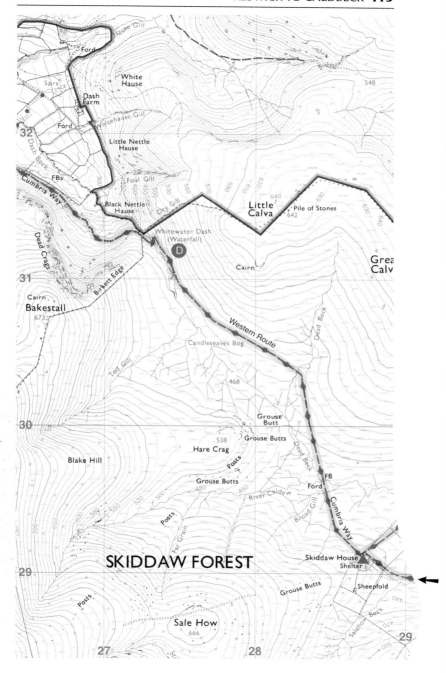

Ford

White
Hause

Spts

Dash
Farm

Hause Gill

548

Whitehause Gill

Ford

Little Nettle
Hause

32

Dash Beck

FBs

Cumbria Way

Foul Gill

Dry Gill

Little
Calva

Pile of Stones
642

640

630

640

630

Black Nettle
Hause

Dead Crags

Whitewater Dash
(Waterfall)

D

Cairn

Grea
Calv

31

Birkett Edge

Cairn
Bakestall
673

Western Route

Dead Beck

Candleseaves Bog

Tod Gill

468

30

Grouse
Butt

538   Grouse Butts

Hare Crag

Blake Hill

Posts

Dead Beck

Grouse Butts

480   460

FB

Ford

Far Grain

Posts

River Caldew

Broad Gill

Cumbria Way

SKIDDAW FOREST

Skiddaw House
Shelter

29

Posts

Grouse Butts

Sheepfold

Salehow Beck

Sale How
666

29

27   28

As the route heads west from Skiddaw House, the view opens out to softer, more

ounded hills and the coast.

one can see how the stone walls snake along, echoing the bends of the beck. Continue on the metalled road to the left, from which there are views out over Bassenthwaite Lake.

At the road **56,** cross straight over to the stile by the gate and take the path signposted to Bassenthwaite, way-marked by a white dot and arrow. The path soon leaves the farm track to turn left by a prominent tree and head off to a stile by a gate in the corner of the field **57**. Here the way divides. The way-marked path leads straight forward for a mile to Bassenthwaite village, but the Cumbria Way turns right beside the fence, signposted to Orthwaite. Stay with the line of the fence to head for the conifer woodland. Go through a gate and continue in the same direction across the next field passing High Close Farm on your left. Just before the woodland **58**, go through the gate on the right and make your way down to the stream, which is crossed on a footbridge. On the opposite bank, take the wide track up to the road, cross straight over and take the path that winds up through the trees beside the beck, signposted Public Bridleway. It leaves the beck to climb steeply to a stile by a gate. The route now follows a farm track that swings round to the right to another stile, and one can again look across to the dark, brooding fells.

Topping a rise, Little Tarn appears down below. At the next gate and stile **59**, where the farm path swings right, do not cross the stile but turn left on the path beside the fence to a ladder stile. Once over this, head downhill, aiming to leave the tarn to your right, and keep to a reasonably high level to avoid the marshy ground at the water's edge. Beyond the tarn, head for a gatepost by a patch of trees, with an old hut beyond it. Cross the stream, go through a metal gate and turn left across the stile in the fence. Head up the field, ignoring a stile on the right. After crossing a stile by a gate, head towards the houses, leaving the field by a stile close to the wire fence on the right **60**.

Turn left along the road, which is now followed for a mile and a half. Here the walk takes on a very different character, with a high beech hedge to the right and a wide prospect of low hills to the left. Topping the hill, Over Water comes into view and now the road can be seen to form a boundary between the green, fertile lands to the west and the sombre fells to the east. At the road junction, continue straight on in the direction of Caldbeck. The road climbs past a reservoir, with the hills of Scotland visible in the far distance. By the top of the climb, coarse moorland grass has crept up to both sides of the road. The road descends to cross a beck, immediately beyond which is a ladder stile on the right **61**. Cross the stile and take the green path beside the wall that goes round the back of the farm buildings. It runs above a little

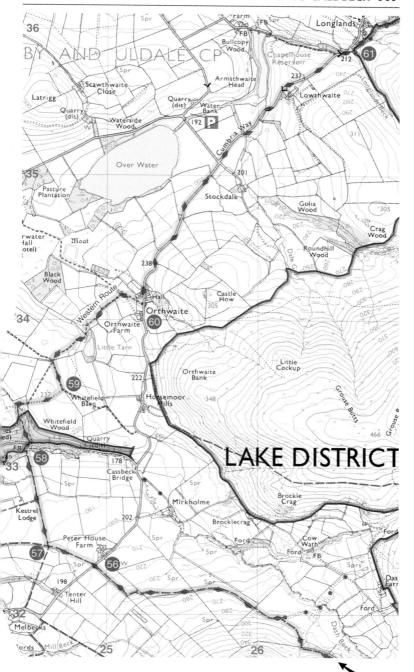

A small farm takes shelter among the trees in the open countryside of the Uldale Fe

beck and a small plantation before leading out onto the open moors. This is excellent, airy walking, with the path cutting a green swathe through the moorland brightened by gorse. Looping round the hillside opens up a panorama that includes the Solway Firth and the hills beyond. The track dips down to ford a stream and then to re-emerge as a stone-surfaced track that continues on the edge of the moor, another lonely area where, apart from the ubiquitous sheep, companions are limited to the occasional curlew and meadow pipit. The surfaced track now leads down past a farm to the road **62** which runs along the appealingly onomatopoeic Burblethwaite Beck.

Turn right up the road which heads off to the attractive settlement of Branthwaite, where the beck is crossed by a handsome stone bridge. In summer the stream attracts flocks of martins which swoop across the water to feed on the clouds of midges and other insects. The little Caldbeck Board School of 1875 appears at the edge of the hamlet before the road goes on to Fell Side. Continue on past all the buildings, then turn right by the very last of them, a fine elegant house (now an Outdoor Education Centre) and turn right

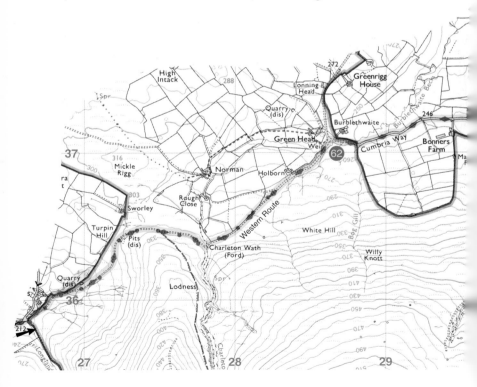

up the public footpath **63**. Cross a stile and join the path of concrete slabs leading up the moor. Wind turbines can be seen up ahead and Caldbeck village lies in sight at the end of a patch of woodland. The track ends at Little Fell Side farm, but the route continues past the farm on a less distinct path heading towards the next farm in the valley, Potts Gill. The route stays on the side of the hill, a little distance from the wall. Pass behind the farm, cross the beck by the footbridge and turn left towards the gate at the edge of the buildings **64**. The path leads round the farm outbuildings to the farm approach road. Turn right on this road, which takes a less than direct route round the fields and over a brook, until it meets the road at Nether Row **55**. Turn left and the two routes are reunited.

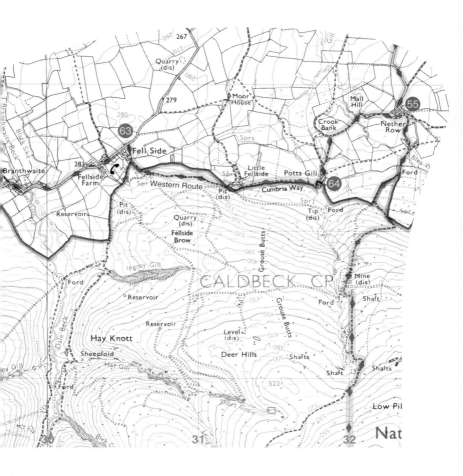

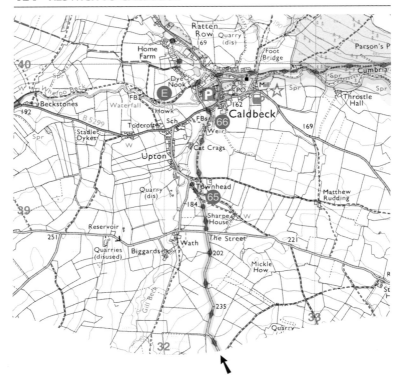

NETHER ROW TO CALDBECK

Carry straight on down the road from Nether Row, cross straight over the road junction, and continue on the narrow lane opposite. At a break in the hedge on the right **65**, turn right by a Cumbria Way sign to cross a stile. Cross the field to a stile to the right of the house – a sign advertises 'Free Range Eggs' and is clearly well justified, for there are hens running everywhere. Cross the track to a stone step stile and continue on the path by the hedge, cross another stile and take the path that dips down through the trees to a stream crossed by a foot-bridge. Follow the path between fences, passing a house with a water-wheel, to the road **66**. Turn right past an old building now housing a clogmaker and blacksmith to reach the centre of Caldbeck. This is an attractive little village, and anyone with time to spare should visit The Howk **E**, a limestone gorge on the Whelpo Beck with the remains of an old bobbin mill. A better preserved watermill, with its breast-shot wheel still intact, can be found behind the church. Built in 1702, this former corn mill now houses workshops, shops and a restaurant.

Traditional stone houses enjoying a fine river view near the bridge at Caldbeck.

Ascent of Skiddaw

Direct return route 5 ½ miles (9 km); circular route 6 miles (10 km)

There are two possibilities here. The first is to take the very clear and well-used path to the summit and return the same way. This leaves the car park **A** and at first uses the Cumbria Way path. Where tracks divide **48**, turn off to the left to take the path heading uphill past the memorial to two Skiddaw shepherds. The route scarcely needs description, it is so well used, its popularity largely due to the fact that it offers the easiest route up any of the high Lakeland peaks, with good walking on its rounded flanks. The path climbs steadily up Jenkin Hill, cutting round the back of the Little Man before turning onto the summit ridge, having reached a height of just over 3000 feet (931 metres).

An alternative route can be used to turn this into a circular walk. The starting point is again the car park **A**, but this time leave by the road, which begins unpromisingly for an ascent by immediately heading off steeply downhill along the side of the plantation. The road passes the impressive Underscar Hotel and views open out over the lake. It continues straight on at the road junction passing a tiny wayside church which, from the outside, could be taken for a village hall. The oak-shaded lane reaches Millbeck where it dips to cross a beck and climbs away again. At the top of the rise **B**, turn right up the footpath signposted to Skiddaw. Turn left through a wooden gate onto a narrow path that leads to the grassy hillside. Take the broad green track on the

Looking out over Keswick from the flanks of Skiddaw.

left which climbs steeply to a stile. Beyond that, the track turns left and then continues straight up the White Stones ridge. At the end of the ridge where it levels out, with superb views over Derwent Water and Bassenthwaite, turn right to pass tiny Carlside Tarn **C**. Here, where paths divide, carry straight on for the final stiff climb to the summit ridge **D**. Carry on along the ridge to the summit cairn itself **E**, then return to **D** and turn left onto the main Skiddaw path, described above, for the descent back to the car park.

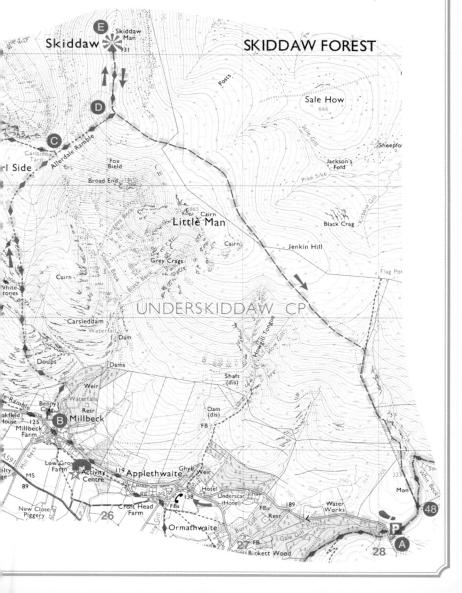

5 CALDBECK TO CARLISLE

via Sebergham and Dalston   *15½ miles (25 km)*

In Caldbeck, cross over the bridge and turn right towards the church **A**. The building shows many changes and developments from the Norman arch in the porch to the eighteenth-century tower. There are a number of finely carved headstones in the churchyard and two are famous: John Peel, the fox hunter, and Mary Robinson, known as Mary of Buttermere. Outside the church is St Kenteigern's well. Continue on the road past the church and where this comes to an end, go through the metal gate and carry straight on along the riverside track. The path rounds a sewage works and heads off into the conifer plantation. Where the path divides, take the path heading uphill to the left **67**. After a steep climb it begins to level out as an obvious, if muddy, track. Eventually it swings right onto firmer ground for a pleasant walk through conifers with a fringe of deciduous trees, another good area to look out for red squirrels.

This section ends at a gate in a fence, and the route now continues straight on, staying close to the top of the field. The two wind turbines, first seen on the last section of the Way, come into view, as does the great expanse of moorland around High Peak. The path runs along beside a line of trees, with a fence down below to the right, eventually

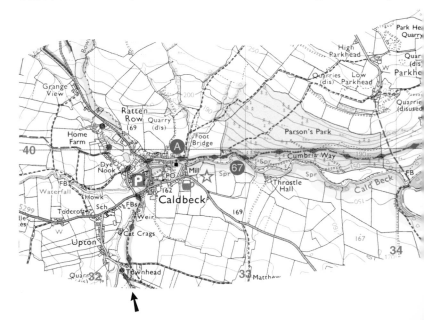

34

heading for a gate beside the prominent clump of trees. Continue along the field with the woodland to the right, then cut diagonally over to the left for a wooden gate in the corner of the fields by the wood. The Way now continues on a more obvious path through the trees in the direction shown by an arrow on the gate. The track runs through a clearing with conifers to the right and more woodland higher up to the left. This is a typical forest road, and on entering the wood it is important to keep an eye open for the turn off it. Look for a pile of stones beside the track with an arrow pointing to a narrow path that plunges steeply downhill through the trees **68**. This is very easy to miss and it is a good idea to take a compass check every now and then: if you find the track turning north then you have come too far.

When the path eventually emerges at the riverbank, turn left on the waterside path, which is liable to be extremely wet and boggy in places. Leaving the wood, keep straight on along the edge of the trees through a series of gates which eventually leads to a broad track that swings away

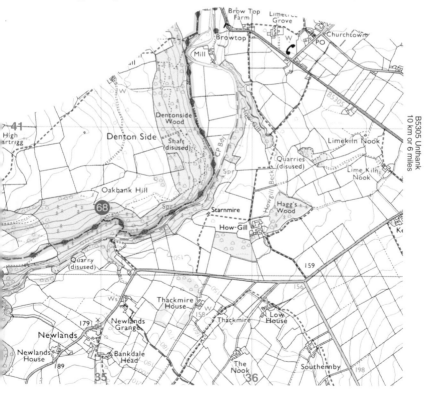

B5305 Unthank
10 km or 6 miles

An old water mill on the Caldew.

to the farm and on to the road **69**. Cross the road bridge over the river, and immediately turn left onto the public bridleway to Sebergham church. Go through the iron gate and follow the clear path that climbs steeply away from the river before turning right to arrive at the vicarage. From here a surfaced lane leads straight to the church **B**, which is a good deal smaller and more modest than the sumptuous vicarage. It does, however, reflect the importance of local dignitaries in a number of elaborate funerary monuments, including an unusual mosaic. One odd feature is an external staircase leading to a tower room above the organ.

Turn left opposite the church onto the bridleway to Bell Bridge. The path passes the very grand entrance to Sebergham Hall, but the house itself remains hidden behind tall hedges. On reaching the road **70**, turn left to cross the river on what is for this area a typically high-arched bridge. On the far side, turn immediately right, cross the stone wall and take the awkward steps down to the field. The Way now follows the bank of the River Caldew, which will be a close companion for most of the rest of the journey. This is very pleasant walking beside the tree-shaded river. A little footbridge crosses an abandoned mill leat and the path keeps to the river bank, with the old mill itself on view to the left. Here there are no problems finding the route as the path proceeds across a series of stiles. Soon a series of jumps and obstacles appear along the way, not intended for over-enthusiastic walkers but as part of an equestrian cross-country course. After crossing a footbridge over a small stream, the scene opens out to attractive meadowland beside the gently meandering Caldew, where the occasional heron eyes its fishy inhabitants, but takes umbrage at the

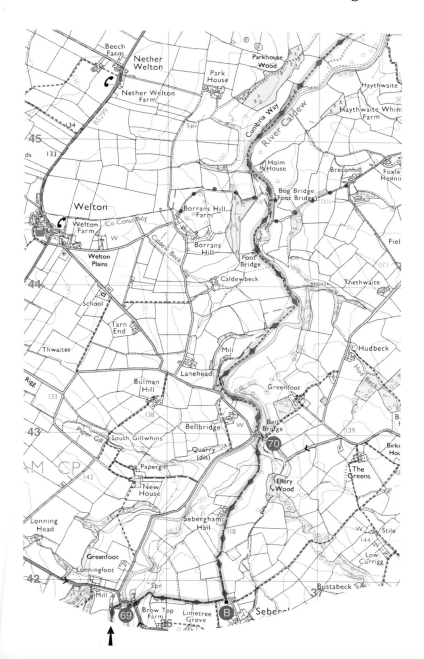

arrival of walkers in its domain, and leaves with a lazy wing flap to take a new, less public perch.

After passing a small conifer plantation, Rose Castle **C** appears across the fields. It is only open to visitors by special arrangement, but it can easily be seen from the walk. This is the formal residence of the Bishops of Carlisle and consists of a grand house and chapel built of local red sandstone and, as a reminder of rougher days, a separate, gaunt peel tower. And rough days they certainly were. The first tower was built by Bishop Halton in the thirteenth century, but only survived until 1322, when it was destroyed by Robert the Bruce. It was rebuilt in the fifteenth century, used as a prison by the Parliamentarians in the Civil War, then recaptured and burned by the Royalists. Restored once again, it narrowly escaped destruction in the Jacobite rebellion of 1745. It is hard to imagine such a violent past in such a tranquil setting. Here the river is crossed by a bridge built of the same rich stone, with two arches over the main stream and a third flood arch. Cross the roadway but not the bridge, then continue on the same bank. The river swings to the right, but the path goes straight forward to briefly rejoin it at the big bend **71**. Continue on to cross a small footbridge to the left and carry straight forward, heading for the left-hand side of the woodland up ahead. Cross a second small bridge and go forward to a kissing gate in the fence – not designed to accommodate walkers and back packs. The fields now are like parkland, graced with fine old oak trees. Head off to the right towards the woodland that surrounds the grand house, now Lime House school. Go through a kissing gate into the woods, and follow the path up to the school drive and leave by a second kissing gate. Continue across the parkland on the obvious track, then turn right on the metalled track signposted to Bridge End **72**. This passes the conspicuously elegant Georgian house, Hawksdale Hall, with its no less attractive gabled outbuildings. Where the road ends, go through the gate on the right and continue along the obvious farm track which curves round to the left. It climbs a little hill which gives a suitable viewpoint for enjoying the parkland. This is very different from the rugged scenery that has dominated so much of the route, a gentle landscape of low contours and studied effects. And now the hills of Lakeland have disappeared out of sight. Go through a gate into the strip of woodland and turn down to the road, where it comes as a shock to arrive at something very like suburbia.

At the roadway **73**, turn right to cross the river on the high-arched sandstone bridge. Follow the road round to the right into the old centre of the village of Buckabank, and turn left by an old mill building onto the road beside the mill stream. This carries straight on through the buildings of a working textile mill, crosses the river and heads up

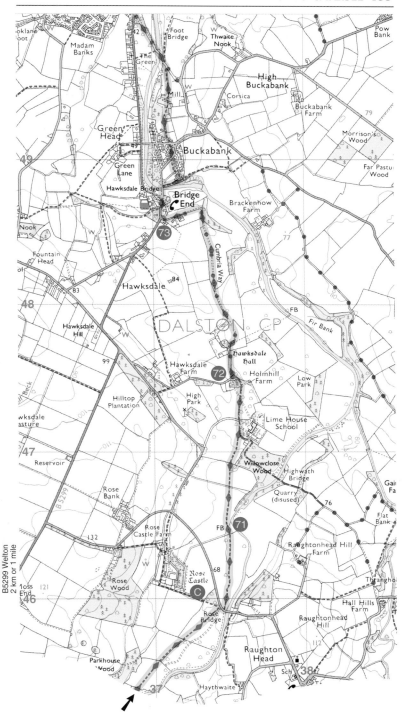

towards the village of Dalston. At the road **74**, turn right. This is a pleasant spot with a small square, a green and a church approached under an unusual sandstone lych gate which is swathed in ivy. The church too is a bit of a surprise, with a complex wooden roof, like something out of a great tithe barn, and a very ornate altar piece. There is also a reminder in the porch that this has been a textile area for a very long time, with a carving of a pair of cropping shears, used for trimming the nap of the cloth. Continue past the church and where the road divides, carry straight on. Immediately beyond the primary school **75**, turn right on the footpath signposted to Cummersdale. This runs round the edge of school playing fields and turns towards the large Nestlé factory which dominates the skyline. Soon, however, the path turns off towards the river again, which occasionally can be glimpsed behind a barrier of willow, hogweed and willow herb. When the river does appear, it flows slow and brown, very different from the dashing young thing encountered earlier. The path plunges through an area of dense, scrubby woodland before reaching a gate and heading off towards a sewage works.

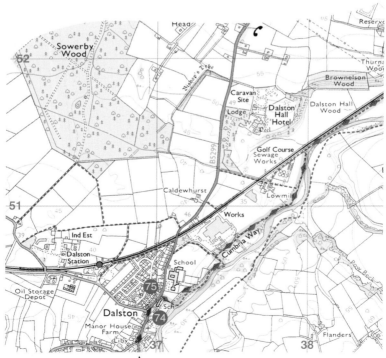

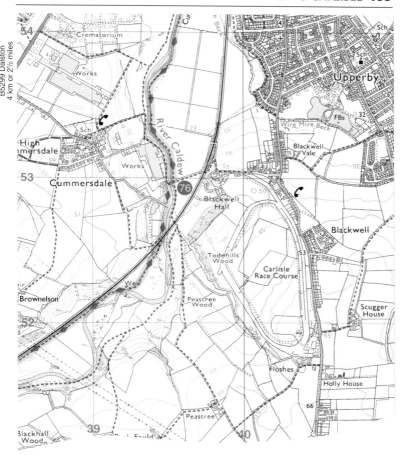

Beyond the works, the river begins to swing away, but the path continues straight on keeping close to the railway. The river eventually loops back again to run close to the edge of the embankment. This section of the path was restored in 1997 following a flood that caused serious erosion. It is hoped that the erosion problem has now been solved, but if problems recur diversion signs will be set in place, and these should always be observed. The path crosses a millstream on a footbridge, and then, just beyond the weir, river and path again diverge. Where they rejoin, the railway crosses the river, but the path continues on the same side to join a road. Just before the factory entrance **76,** turn right to cross a footbridge and then left onto the riverside path that will now take you into the outskirts of Carlisle, which can be seen up ahead dominated by tall mill chimneys. This is a narrow path between river and fields, which becomes more open as it gets nearer the houses. An old mill stands by an immense weir, and the path now continues on the river bank by a strip of parkland separating it from the houses. The riverside path soon comes to an end, and with it the Cumbria Way. But most walkers will not want to be stranded there on the outskirts, so, to reach the city centre, take the road past the gas holders, one of which has a splendidly ornate framework, and cross over the bridge to the road junction. Turn left and continue to the city centre.

Carlisle makes a fitting end to the walk, with the remains of its castle and its resplendent cathedral, much damaged during the Civil War, but still retaining wonderfully carved misericords, an immensely rich east window and reminders of an austere Norman grandeur. The quiet of the cathedral close is as good a place as any to sit and think back to the very different peace and tranquillity of fell and valley along the Cumbria Way.

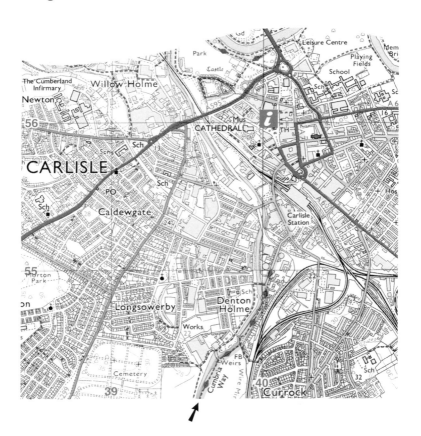

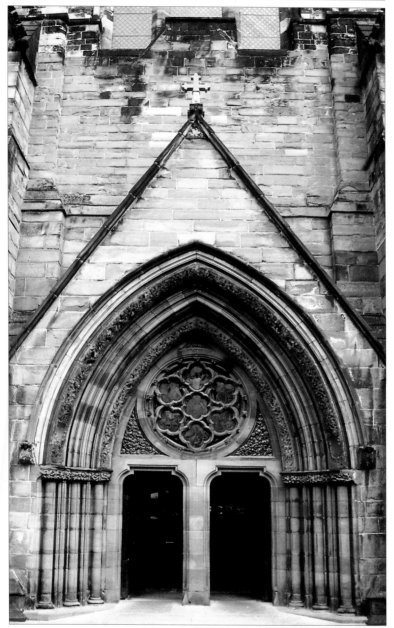

The startling red of the sandstone produces a striking effect at the entrance to Carlisle Cathedral.

USEFUL INFORMATION

Transport

Information on transport to and from the Cumbria Way can be obtained from local tourist information centres.

Rail

Ulverston can be reached via Oxenholme on the main line and at the end of the journey Carlisle is on a main line route.

Rail Enquiries 0345 484 950

Coach

All coach enquiries from National Express: 0990 808 080
    Also Cumbria Journey Planner Enquiry Line for all information on bus and rail: 01228 606 000

Ferries

Coniston Water

Coniston launch	Coniston	Tel. 015394 36216
Steam Yacht *Gondola*	Coniston Pier	Tel. 015394 41288

Derwent Water

Keswick launch	Keswick	Tel. 017687 72263

Accommodation

Information on hotels, guest houses, bed and breakfast and camping facilities can be obtained from tourist information centres. The publication *Stilwell's National Trail Companion* also gives useful information and a small booklet, *Cumbria Way Accommodation Guide* by Philip Dubock, is available from MIWay Publishing, PO Box 2, Keswick, Cumbria, CA12 4GA or from tourist information centres.

Youth Hostels on or near the Cumbria Way

Arnside Oakfield Lodge, Redhills Road, Arnside, Carnforth, Lancashire, LA5 0AT. Tel: 01524 761781. GR 452783.
Borrowdale Longthwaite, Borrowdale, Keswick, CA12 5XE. Tel: 017687 77257. GR 254142.
Carrock Fell High Row Cottage, Haltcliffe, Hesket Newmarket, Wigton, CA7 8JT. Tel: 016974 78325. GR 358355.
Coniston Holly How, Far End, Coniston, LA21 8DD. Tel: 015394 41323. GR 302980.
Copper Mines House, Coniston, LA21 8HP. Tel: 015394 41261. GR 289986.
Elterwater Elterwater, Ambleside, LA22 9HX. Tel: 015394 37245. GR 327046.
Keswick Station Road, Keswick, CA12 5LH. Tel: 017687 72484. GR 267235.
Langdale High Close, Loughrigg, Ambleside LA22 9HJ. Tel: 015394 37313. GR 338052.
Skiddaw Skiddaw House, Bassenthwaite, Keswick, Cumbria CA12 4QX. No telephone – contact Carrock Fell Youth Hostel. GR 288291. Facilites are limited; postal bookings only.

There is no youth hostel in Carlisle but YHA have alternative arrangements in place with the University of Northumbria to use their 'Old Brewery Residences' in the centre of Carlisle during July, August and early September.

For any enquiries contact YHA Northern Region, PO Box 11, Matlock, Derbyshire, DE4 2XA. Tel: 01629 825850.

Camping Barns on or near the Cumbria Way

Catbells Barn	NY243208	on the Way
Eagles Nest Barn	NY258259	2 miles from the Way
Hudscales Barn	NY331375	just off the Way
Fell End Barn	SD239881	2 miles from the Way
Dinah Hoggus Barn	NY259150	on the Way

For an information leaflet, write to Keswick Information Centre, 31 Lake Road, Keswick, CA12 5DQ. Booking through Lake District National Park Authority.

TOURIST INFORMATION CENTRES

Cumbria Tourist Board, Ashleigh, Holly Road, Windermere, LA23 2AQ. Tel: 015394 44444.

Ambleside: Old Court House, Church Street, Ambleside, LA22 0BT. Tel: 015394 32582.

Carlisle, Old Town Hall, Green Market, Carlisle, CA3 8JH. Tel: 01228 512444.

*****Coniston:** Ruskin Avenue, Coniston, LA21 8EH. Tel: 015394 41533.

Keswick: Moot Hall, Market Square, Keswick, CA12 5JR. Tel: 017687 72645.

*****Seatoller:** Seatoller Barn, Borrowdale, Keswick, CA12 5XN. Tel: 017687 77294.

Ulverston: Coronation Hall, County Square, Ulverston, LA12 7LZ. Tel: 01229 587120.

*****Waterhead:** Main Car Park, Waterhead, Ambleside, LA22 0EN. Tel: 015394 32729.

*seasonal opening

LAKE DISTRICT NATIONAL PARK

The Lake District National Park has a ranger service which covers quite a large part of the Cumbria Way.
National Park Ranger Service. Tel: 01539 724555
Northern Ranger Services at Blencathra. Tel: 017687 79633

There is a long distance Weatherline and Fell Top Forecast on 017687 75757.

Lake District National Park Information Centres on or near the Cumbria Way are at:
Coniston – Ruskin Avenue
Waterhead
Seatoller Barn, Borrowdale

USEFUL ADDRESSES

British Trust for Ornithology, The Nunnery, Thetford, Norfolk, IP24 2PU. Tel: 01842 750050.

Cumbria Wildlife Trust, Church Street, Ambleside, LA22 0BU.

English Heritage (North), Bessie Surtees House, 41–44 Sandhill, Newcastle-upon-Tyne, BE13 3JF.

English Nature, Blackwell, Bowness, Windermere, LA23 3JR. Tel: 015394 45286.

Lake District National Park Authority, Murley Ross, Oxenholme Road, Kendal, LA9 7RL. Tel. 01539 724555.

National Trust, The Hollens, Grasmere, Ambleside, LA22 9QZ. Tel: 015394 35599.

Ordnance Survey, Romsey Road, Maybush, Southampton, SO16 4GU.

Ramblers' Association, 1–5 Wandworth Road, London, SW8 2XX. Tel: 0171 582 6878.

Royal Society for the Protection of Birds, The Lodge, Sandy, Beds. The Youth Hostels Assocation, Trevelyan House, 8 St Stephen's Hill, St Albans, Herts, AL1 2DY. Tel: 01727 55215.

Northern Region: P.O. Box 11, Matlock, Derbyshire, DE4 2XA. Tel: 01629 825850.

ORDNANCE SURVEY MAPS COVERING THE CUMBRIA WAY

Landranger Maps
(Scale 1: 50,000)

85 Carlisle & The Solway Firth
90 Penrith, Keswick & Ambleside Area
96 Barrow-in-Furness & South Lakeland Area

Outdoor Leisure Maps
(Scale 1:25,000)

4 The English Lakes North Western Area
5. The English Lakes North Eastern Area
6 The English Lakes South Western Area
7 The English Lakes South Eastern Area

Pathfinder Maps
(Scale 1:25,000)

558 Carlisle (East) and Castle Carrock

BIBLIOGRAPHY

Barringer, Christopher, *The Lake District*, Willow, 1984

Bragg, Melvyn, *Land of the Lakes*, Secker & Warburg, 1983

Dunn, Michael, *The Lake District*, David & Charles, 1988

Joy, David, *The Lake Counties* (A Regional History of the Railways of Great Britain series) David & Charles, 1983

Marshall, J.D. & Davies-Shiel, M., *The Lake District At Work Past and Present*, David & Charles, 1971

Millward, Roy & Robinson, Adrian, *The Lake District*, Eyre Methuen, 1970

Nicholson, Norman, *The Lake District: An Anthology*, Penguin, 1978

–, *Portrait of the Lakes*, Robert Hale, 1972

Prosser, Robert, *Geology Explained in the Lake District*, David & Charles, 1977

Rollinson, William, *Life & Tradition in the Lake District*, J. M. Dent, 1974

Taylor, Tim Page, *A Field Guide to the Lake District & its Environs*, Dalesman, 1984

Wyatt, John, *The Lake District National Park Guide*, Webb & Bower/Michael Joseph, 1987

PLACES TO VISIT ON OR NEAR THE CUMBRIA WAY

Ulverston Laurel & Hardy Museum, 4c Upper Brook Street.

Heron Glass, The Gill.

Cumbria Crystal, Lightburn Road.

Ulverston Heritage Centre, Lower Brook Street.

Coniston The Ruskin Museum, Yewdale Road.

Brantwood (by water)

Steam yacht *Gondola*, Pier Cottage

Skelwith Bridge Kirkstone Galleries

Lingholm Gardens

Keswick Museum and Art Gallery, Fitz Park, Station Road.

The Cumberland Pencil Factory, Southey Works, Greta Bridge

Lake District National Park Centre.

Caldbeck Priests Mill

Carlisle The Regimental Museum of the Border Regiment & The King's Own Royal Border Regiment Museum, The Castle.

Cathedral

Guildhall Museum, Green Market.

The Citadel and West Walls

Carlisle Castle (EH)

Tullie House Museum and Art Gallery, Castle Street.